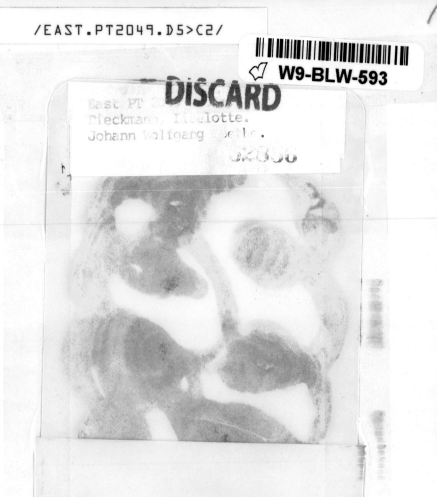

Oakton Community College

Morton Grove, Illinois

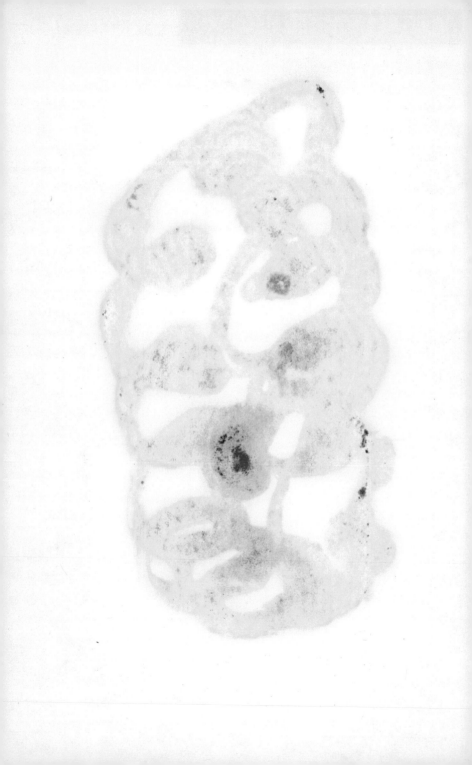

TWAYNE'S WORLD AUTHORS SERIES

A Survey of the World's Literature

Sylvia Bowman, Indiana University

GENERAL EDITOR

GERMANY

Ulrich Weisstein, Indiana University

EDITOR

Johann Wolfgang Goethe

TWAYNE'S WORLD AUTHORS SERIES (TWAS)

*The purpose of TWAS is to survey the major writers
—novelists, dramatists, historians, poets, philosophers,
and critics—of the nations of the world. Among the
national literatures covered are those of Australia,
Canada, China, Eastern Europe, France, Germany,
Greece, India, Italy, Japan, Latin America, the Netherlands, New Zealand, Poland, Russia, Scandinavia,
Spain, and the African nations, as well as Hebrew,
Yiddish, and Latin Classical literatures. This survey
is complemented by Twayne's United States Authors
Series and English Authors Series.*

*The intent of each volume in these series is to present
a critical-analytical study of the works of the writer;
to include biographical and historical material that
may be necessary for understanding, appreciation,
and critical appraisal of the writer; and to present all
material in clear, concise English—but not to vitiate
the scholarly content of the work by doing so.*

Johann Wolfgang Goethe

By LISELOTTE DIECKMANN

Washington University

TWAYNE PUBLISHERS

A DIVISION OF G. K. HALL & CO., BOSTON

Library of Congress Cataloging in Publication Data

Dieckmann, Liselotte.
    Johann Wolfgang Goethe.

    (Twayne's world author series, TWAS 292. Germany)
    Bibliography: p.
    1.   Goethe, Johann Wolfgang von, 1749-1832.
PT2049.D5   831'.6   73-20264
ISBN   0-8057-2378-1

For my children and grandchildren

Contents

Preface

Johann Wolfgang Goethe (1749–1832) was, for the longest time, considered by his German speaking readers as being in a class with Shakespeare and Dante, i.e., as the greatest author in the German-speaking world. Until fairly recently[1] this position remained undisputed. Today, however, he is not widely read, and his works are no longer well known; in fact, many young Germans consider Goethe's greatness to be a myth and refuse to read him at all. It is, therefore, not inappropriate to speak of a crisis which his fame, unchallenged up to now, is presently undergoing. For each great author a re-evaluation of his work will at times occur.[2] This is a prerequisite if an author's work is to remain alive. This generation has criteria measuring greatness, which may differ from those of the generation before it, and an author is important only insofar as he is read and loved.

At present the objections to Goethe's work and personality are, in part, based on Marxist or somewhat more general sociological and political arguments. It can be said, with some justification, that Goethe was neither socially nor politically oriented, that he was a highly developed individualist who turned from the effects of the French revolution because they were bloody and, in his opinion, fruitless. Whereas his younger, romantic contemporaries moved away from him because, during the wars against Napoleon, he proved to be insufficiently nationalistic or patriotic, others, such as Beethoven, despised him because he appeared to be servile to the aristocracy. There are still other points on which he is criticized. His great efforts to collect and classify all sorts of natural objects is regarded as pedantic, and his insertion of generalizing statements on life into his works is considered pompous. Moreover, Goethe is seen as a self-important man who tried to dominate the intellectual life of his time and, not being able to rule his younger contemporaries, withdrew from them in disdain.

This book does not intend to invalidate such observations. There is, naturally, some truth in them, and polemics will not convince anyone. Instead, I will try to lead the reader to a somewhat deeper understanding of the man and his work, avoiding both present-day objections and previous over-evaluations of a man whose mind embraced a vast amount of knowledge, and who wrote remarkable poetry. Goethe was disliked by some of his contemporaries and overly admired by others. He exerted an immense influence on the latter part of the nineteenth and the first part of the twentieth century.

The need for a re-evaluation of Goethe's work, however, is hindered not only by the objections mentioned above but, above all, by the exaggerated praise he has received from earlier critics. Goethe criticism has been handicapped from the beginning by the fact that Goethe lived on into the nineteenth century and into the period of the rising bourgeoisie, which chose him as its undisputed leader in poetic and philosophical matters. Since he liked in his later years to educate his public and raise its level of aesthetic understanding as well as moral judgment, his words were taken as ultimate wisdom, quoted out of context, and considered an ideal guide for human behavior. Some of his characters, too, were looked upon as models to be imitated. For anyone trained in the German school system it will always be difficult to disregard this one-sided image of Goethe. However, to gain an over-all judgment on so complex a figure, we must also emphasize those sides of his genius which were brushed over by this criticism. His profound psychological insights, his sense of tragedy, his amazing understanding of life processes are accented in this study, as well as his masterly use of symbols and poetic forms. The latter particularly have always been underestimated since form was not considered his foremost achievement.

The banality characteristic of much of Goethe criticism mentioned above is hard to cope with. If I have omitted too many of the standard ideas on Goethe, it was done for the sake of what I hope to be a fairly fresh approach. To consider Goethe a "bourgeois" writer is rather ludicrous in view of the fact that his characters almost always belong to the aristocracy and that, if he describes a "bourgeois," he does so most often with contempt. He is, in this respect, very much the heir of the French eighteenth-century authors, from Voltaire to Rousseau, who moved in aristocratic circles and found an echo to their writings among them. Goethe does not see the culture of the future as resting in the hands of the bourgeoisie, but rather in the aristocratic leisure class to which he was always strongly attracted and which he considered truly productive. Many reproach him for this attitude —and we know that Goethe himself was not always happy about the choice he had made. In fact, he had strong reservations. Whether we, personally, like or dislike this attitude is an irrelevant question. We have to accept it as a biographical fact and should look at his poetic work on a level that precludes our own political or social bias.

This book does not pretend to contribute to Goethe scholarship; it is rather meant as an introduction, addressed to a reader unfamiliar with Goethe's works, and intended as a guide to close reading. Recent scholarly controversies will be largely avoided, and scholarly references are kept to a minimum. While the book was very difficult to write, mainly because of the proliferation of Goethe scholarship, it does not have any ambitions beyond its avowed purpose of helping the twentieth-century reader to find his way through the maze of Goethe's writings. If that goal is achieved, I will be satisfied.

The book is not divided according to periods in Goethe's life and work, but rather discusses various types of works, mostly, but not exclusively, literary. The purpose of this division is to point out Goethe's innovations in, or improvements on, the literary genres then existing. On the other hand, such a division implies that, with each new genre, the discussion has to start early in his life and proceed in a roughly chronological order. While trying to avoid repetitions in the biographical data, I feel that this method is the only one by which a tedious biographical presentation can be avoided, as each chapter enlarges on the intellectual and literary horizons presented in the preceding ones. At least in intention, each new chapter should thus add another concentric circle around the core of his personality. Cross-references will help to keep the chronological perspective in mind. Each chapter will start with some general considerations and then give a close reading of some of Goethe's best writings in a given genre. Thus it is hoped that the perspective of his life and time is kept in focus while single works are given a closer scrutiny.

As a last, but to me very important, consideration I should like to mention the inescapable insight that it is presumptuous to write on an author as complex and difficult as Goethe who left a large body of works and infinitely more unfinished projects, plans, and ideas. Even a good Goethe scholar will not be able to read all this material, in addition to the prodigious amount of secondary material on any number of topics. Significant omissions and subjective preferences are unavoidable in a short study of this kind, and the lack of completeness and, in part, even competence made my task almost overwhelming. I apologize to all those who could have handled the problem much better.

LISELOTTE DIECKMANN

Chronology

(For the works, the date indicates the year of publication, not the date of inception or completion.)

1749 Born in Frankfurt, son of an upper-class, educated and well-to-do bourgeois, and grandson of the Mayor.

1765– Student at Leipzig.
1768

1768– Frankfurt.
1770

1770– Law student in Strasbourg. Meets Herder.
1771

1771– Attorney in Frankfurt.
1772

1772 Wetzlar.

1773– Frankfurt. *Götz von Berlichingen, Die Leiden des jungen*
1775 *Werther* (The Sorrows of Young Werther), many poems. *Clavigo. Stella.*

1775 In November, he moves to Weimar at the invitation of Duke Karl August.

1776 Member of the secret council. Becomes Prime Minister.

1777 Trip to the Harz mountains. Poem "Harzreise im Winter" (Harz Mountain Trip).

1784 Discovers the intermaxillary bone.

1785 Starts studying botany.

1786– Trip to Italy, *Iphigenie auf Tauris, Egmont, Torquato*
1788 *Tasso, Römische Elegien* (Roman Elegies).

1789 His son August is born to Christiane Vulpius.

1790 First edition of his *Gesammelte Werke* (Collected Works) in 8 volumes. *Metamorphose der Pflanzen* (Metamorphosis of Plants). Trip to Venice. *Venezianische Epigramme* (Venetian Epigrams).

1791 Becomes director of the Weimar Theater.

1792   Begins to prepair a new edition of his works (7 volumes to 1799). *Kampagne in Frankreich* (The Campaign in France).

1793   *Der Bürgergeneral* (The Bourgeois General). *Reineke Fuchs. Belagerung von Mainz* (The Siege of Mainz).

1794   Beginning of his friendship with Schiller.

1795   *Die Horen* (The Horae). *Unterhaltungen deutschen Ausgewanderten* (Conversations of German Emigrants). *Märchen* (Fairy Tale).

1796   *Xenien* (with Schiller). *Hermann und Dorothea. Wilhelm Meisters Lehrjahre* (Wilhelm Meister's Apprenticeship).

1797   *Balladen.*

1798–   *Propyläen* (a journal mainly concerned with art).
1800

1803   *Die Natürliche Tochter* (The Natural Daughter).

1805   Schiller's death.

1806   French occupation of Weimar. He marries Christiane Vulpius.

1808   Publication of *Faust, Eine Tragödie* (Faust I). Collection of his *Gesammelte Werke (12 volumes)*. Meets Napoleon in Erfurt.

1809   *Die Wahlverwandtschaften* (Elective Affinities).

1810   *Farbenlehre* (Theory of Colors).

1812   Meets Beethoven.

1814   Trip to the Main and Rhine. Meets Marianne von Willemer.

1815   Second trip to the Main and Rhine. *Gesammelte Werke in zwanzig Bänden.*

1816   Death of Christiane.

1817   End of his work as director of the Weimar Theater.

1819   *Der West-östliche Divan* (West-Eastern Divan). Some scenes of *Faust* performed in Berlin.

1821   *Wilhelm Meisters Wanderjahre* (Wilhelm Meister's Years of Wandering), Part I.

1823   "Trilogie der Leidenschaft" ("An Werther," "Elegie," "Aussöhnung") (usually called: Marienbad Elegy). Eckermann comes to Weimar.

1826   Prepares final edition of his works (*Ausgabe Letzter Hand*) in 40 volumes (last edition published by Goethe himself). *Novelle.*

Chronology

1831 Finishes *Der Tragödie Zweiter Theil* (Faust II), which is published posthumously in the above edition of his works.

1832 Death.

Translations Used

Unless otherwise stated, the translations are my own. I have used the following translations:

Elective Affinities, translated by Elizabeth Mayer, Chicago; Regnery, 1963 (quoted as "Mayer.")

Faust I and *II*, translated by Charles E. Passage, New York; Bobbs-Merrill, Indianapolis, 1965 (quoted as "Passage.")

Iphigenia in Tauris, translated by Charles E. Passage, New York; Ungar, 1966 (quoted as "Passage.")

Torquato Tasso, translated by Charles E. Passage, New York; Ungar, 1966 (quoted as "Passage.")

The Permanent Goethe, edited by Thomas Mann, New York; Dial Press, 1948 (quoted as "Permanent Goethe.") The poems in this collection are translated by several authors.

CHAPTER 1

Biography and Autobiography

I Biography

GOETHE'S life, seen in its external circumstances, was a happy one, free from want, well protected by family and superiors, and filled with admiring friends. The fact that Goethe himself often considered it to be difficult and hard to bear constitutes the inevitable dichotomy between the outward appearance of ease and comfort and the personal experience of unfulfilled desires, frustrated aspirations, and lonely despair. The two aspects complement each other and can never be separated in any honest discussion of Goethe's personality.

The course of Goethe's external life is quickly told. Born into a well-to-do upper-middle-class family, the grandson of the mayor of the free *Reichsstadt* Frankfurt and the son of a well-read and idle bourgeois, he was largely educated by his own father. He was then sent to the university to receive a law degree. None of his many intellectual pursuits shows itself less in his works than his legal studies, which he undertook to satisfy his father. He completed his degree at the University of Strasbourg, where he indulged in many interests other than those prescribed by his academic studies. He met there, among others, Johann Gottfried Herder, who introduced him to the most recent literary and artistic trends and helped considerably to make his stay in Strasbourg one of his most fruitful experiences. Having gained, after his return to Frankfurt, great fame through the publication of his play *Götz von Berlichingen* he accepted a position as legal councillor in Wetzlar. The literary result of his stay there, the novel *The Sorrows of Young Werther*, gave additional prestige to his name and won for him an offer from the young ruler of the small duchy of Sachsen-Weimar, Karl-August, to come to Weimar, if only temporarily. A warm friendship developed quickly between the Duke and the poet, which was to remain more or less intact throughout their lives. Goethe went to Weimar when he was barely twenty-six years old and died there at the age of eighty-two. He worked with and for the prince in matters of administration, he adorned the court and attracted other poets and thinkers to it. For a while he was the director of the court theater and he quietly pursued his own scientific and aesthetic interests. As he grew older, he developed from an excitable and rebellious young man into a stately, orderly, and almost pedantic sage who was revered throughout Europe and first admired, but later mocked, by the young Romanticists.

In the German mind, Goethe's life has taken on an exemplary quality and a kind of mythical image, which was greatly enhanced by his own careful way of keeping diaries, preserving letters and writing several autobiographical works. The cult of his personality overshadowed for many years the critical understanding of his works, and we are now, one hundred and forty years after his death, just at the beginning of a genuine understanding and evaluation of his literary merits. We have to free ourselves not only from the admiration of his personality, which must have been imposing and impressive, but also from the ingrained habit of quoting him out of context, thereby turning him into a sage whose most famous lines often appear trivial except in the mouths of those characters who utter them.

We must also see in a new perspective Goethe's many loves, which strangely impressed the bourgeois society of the nineteenth century. Those who seem almost to have gained a vicarious love experience by dwelling on his amorous adventures forgot how common it was in the eighteenth century to love easily and often. Goethe's love affairs are, in some respects, remarkably uninteresting. He was a very normal man who fell in love with simple girls and fled when they tried to tie him down. With few exceptions, his love was returned. There is nothing strange in these affairs. (His long and agonizing relationship with a woman much older than he was, Charlotte von Stein, is an exception.) They were valuable to him as a man and poet. What matters to us is their reflections in poetry—but by the time Goethe wrote his love-poems, which are often profound, mysterious, and filled with his very special sense of the "demonic"[1] quality of life, the original love-story no longer interested him. He had the great

gift of being able to free himself of his own emotions by transforming them into art.[2]

II   *Autobiography*

Aside from the bare facts of Goethe's life just related, we must
consider the vast amount of intellectual activity which made
Goethe into the universal figure he became. We can discuss it
here only in its broadest aspects, since his reading, studying,
note-taking, translating, his correspondence and his friendships,
and his discourses, both written and oral, with many famous men
fill many volumes. Anyone who has visited Goethe's home in
Weimar and has seen his collections of books, butterflies, rocks,
ancient statues, etc., realizes that there is no end to the material
that went into his intellectual makeup. His encounters with the
world were undertaken by an ever curious, alert and very perceptive mind, which was open to stimulation by almost anything
it found.

It must be kept in mind, however, that Goethe's was always a
poetic imagination which colored even his most scientific efforts.
When he called his autobiography "Fiction and Truth," he characterized not only this particular work but also his excursions
into biology, geology and physics. His mind was poetically
creative no matter to what field he addressed himself, and if he
erred from a scientific viewpoint (as he sometimes did), we can
see his imagination at odds with his reasoning, whose defeat he
preferred to the triumph of rational abstraction.

Aside from this openness toward the world, and perhaps as a
compensatory force, we see the poet meditating upon himself.
We possess not only a number of autobiographical works such
as *Dichtung und Wahrheit* (Fiction and Truth), *Die italienische
Reise* (The Italian Journey) and the reports on his participation
in the wars following the French Revolution,[3] but also diaries,
letters and notes.

Goethe's diaries begin in the year 1775, at the time of a trip
to Switzerland. They were interrupted for a short time, but then
regularly continued when he set out for Weimar. Whereas the
earlier entries are long and descriptive, the later diaries contain
very brief accounts of his daily doings, a notation on books he
read or persons he saw—in short, simply a brief memo to himself which enabled him to recall his activities which were numer-

ous and vast. None, however, are in any sense introspective. To reread them must have meant for him to be reminded of incidents in his life or observations he had made. His more extensive autobiographies were written many years after the events and composed from letters and diary-entries of one kind or another. They indicate, as clearly as the diaries, the real objective of this enormous effort, namely to keep his life together.

The strongest motivation for writing down so much about himself may well have been Goethe's sense of being a unique, enormously gifted person whose life should be known to his contemporaries as well as to later generations. However, we should not consider this desire as showing outrageous vanity. It is, rather, born out of an awe of being endowed with such gifts, a respect for the "demonic powers" which had made him the man he was, and the desire to keep for posterity the image of a man who often felt misunderstood during his lifetime.

Goethe's autobiographies were written late in life.[4] They show as little introspection as the diaries. Like all of his works, they are both imaginative and realistic. They show his reactions to the world more clearly than his own troubled psyche, although the latter is never lost sight of. He never asked himself *why* or *how* he reacted to the world, but rather *to what* he reacted. His mind thus kept a firm grip on his environment and did not lose itself in his own feelings. If his accounts were not as well written as they are, we might accuse the author of lack of feeling. The external events, large or small, are recorded in these pages, and Goethe's love of detail and accuracy is greater than his interest in his own psychological reactions. We are reading, in these books, more about the world that surrounded their author than about the author himself. If—as happens rarely enough— a situation is selected out of a certain sense of vanity, it is treated so objectively that the vanity becomes unobtrusive and the situation itself remains interesting. Goethe regarded his entire work as fragments of one great confession.[5] But this statement needs clarification, for although he speaks primarily about himself, he hardly reveals himself. Unlike his younger romantic friends, he concealed his own feelings which, by the time he spoke of them, had already been transformed into poetic statements.

In the following pages, I will discuss the various autobiographical works in chronological order rather than the order of their composition. This method should enable us to discern the important facets of his life. There is no room in this short presentation for a thorough discussion of his methods of writing biography which, in his particular case, have been quite insufficiently studied.[6]

III *Of My Life: Truth and Fiction*

This work covers Goethe's life from his birth to the year 1775, when he received the invitation to go to Weimar. It consists of twenty books, five each to a Part. The three first Parts were written, rather rapidly, in 1822–1823, while the last Part lagged and was published only after the author's death.

At the time Goethe undertook to write this book (the *Italian Journey* had already been written in 1814–1816) his youth had long become history. In the *Preface* to the work, he quotes in toto a letter by a friend who, contemplating Goethe's latest twelve-volume edition of his works (1808), begs him to explain to his audience their interconnections and continuity. The letter was fabricated by Goethe, it is a "fiction" in the sense suggested by the title.[7] While he had received many pleas for a presentation of his life, these did not constitute his true motive for wishing to write the autobiography. In the course of the *Preface*, he describes the enormous difficulties which such a task implies and comes to the following conclusion, which reveals his actual purpose:

It seems to be the foremost task of a biography to represent a man in his historical situation and to show in which ways the whole contemporary scene hinders him or furthers him, how he formed a view of man and the world from it, and how, if he is an artist, poet or writer, he reflects it. For this purpose, however, something barely attainable is required, namely that the individual know himself and his century—himself inasmuch as he has kept his identity under all circumstances, and his century inasmuch as the stream which carries him along, willingly or unwillingly, determines and forms him, so that one can say that anyone born only ten years earlier or later would have become, as far as his own formation and his effect on the outside world are concerned, a completely different person.

Clearly, the author set for himself the immense task of analyzing both his own potential (he likes to call it, after Leibniz, his "entelechy") and the mutual effect which the environment and the individual have upon one another. Environment, however, is taken in the broadest possible sense, including both the closest ties (family and friends) and the largest aspects (political and cultural events). The interrelatedness of man's intellectual and emotional self on the one hand, with the changing historical circumstances on the other, is the subject of the book. How does he go about it?

If Goethe wished to present to his nineteenth-century audience a living image of what kind of child and young man he had been, he does not say so, but rather starts out as if he were writing a novel:

On August 28, 1749, at noon, as the bells were ringing twelve o'clock, I was born in Frankfurt on the Main. The constellation was fortunate: The sun stood in the sign of Virgo, and culminated for the day; Jupiter and Venus looked at it sympathetically, and Mercury not adversely; Saturn and Mars were indifferent. Only the moon, which was full, exerted the power of his hostile light, all the more since it had just entered its planetary hour. It therefore opposed my birth, which could not take place until that hour had passed. These positive aspects, which the astrologers considered with great favor, may well have been responsible for my survival . . .

As the beginning of a novel, these words indicate the importance of the future hero of the work. As the beginning of an autobiography, however, the emphasis is probably not intended to be on his own importance, but rather on the strange mixture of destiny and accident into which this particular human being was born. The role of the astrological hour is but a symbol of what Goethe called his destiny (*Bestimmung*), and to which he always opposed that part of his mental makeup which, he felt, had been the result of his own endeavor and self-education.

What has been said so far should indicate Goethe's honest attempt to show himself, not by exploring his mind, heart or soul, but rather by examining the changing world in which he, a changing and yet identical self, was placed. He and his world are inextricably interwoven and must by necessity elucidate one another. In his novel *Wilhelm Meister*, he handled the problem of presenting a character in its relationship to its environment in a similar way—both works express his fundamental belief that man is an individual growing in a benign or hostile environment, changing it or changed by it, as the case may be.

As *Fiction and Truth* is not a confession or a study in depth psychology, the modern reader may miss the psychological depth of such works as St. Augustine's or Rousseau's *Confessions*. Instead, the work gives a lively image of eighteenth-century life in a Free City; it describes historical events, such as the solemn crowning of a German emperor in Frankfurt or the French occupation of Frankfurt during the Seven Years War. It never fails to mention the historical-political causes of cultural events or personal attitudes. And it views with profound concern the smooth superficialities of bourgeois life as opposed to the "strangely mistaken ways which, in reality, undermine bourgeois society": "How many families had I observed who, through bankruptcy, divorce, seductions, murders, thefts, poisoning were either ruined or subsisted pitifully on the margin of society" (Trunz, VIII, 285).

Despite Goethe's reticence to speak about his own feelings, there are always moments when the reader is allowed a glimpse into the depth of his emotional life. In speaking of a light and fleeting passion, the author gives us such an insight. When he loses the girl as a result of his unfortunate habit of torturing her heart, he writes: "I really had lost her. The violence with which I avenged my mistake on myself, by raging in many senseless ways against my physical nature in order to harm my moral one, has contributed much to the physical ills through which I lost some of the best years of my life; in fact I might have perished from my loss, if my poetical talent, with its healing powers, had not proven itself to be particularly helpful" (*ibid.*, p. 284).

Undoubtedly, Goethe did not consider himself capable of harnessing his talent at will when he got into emotional trouble, but he saw himself as a desperate and unwise person who—almost unknowingly—found a cure for his desperate state in being able to write. What cured him was not the description of his ills, but rather the need to present a "case"—such as his own—concisely and objectively. What his friend Schiller has called the instinct of form (*Formtrieb*) was, in many instances of personal despair and rage, Goethe's psychological salvation. Goethe's tendency to find a psychological cure in writing poetry has often been misunderstood as an expression of the self, whereas it was, in reality, the generalization and objectification of a personal experience, lifted by means of a strong and earnest sense of concise form, out of, and away from, the realm of personal experience.[8]

This needs to be emphasized not only in regard to Goethe's "self-expression" in his poems and plays, but particularly in view of his autobiographical works. We are dealing with works of art (fiction) in the first place, and with an historical account (truth) only in the second. Whereas the original subtitle was *Truth and Fiction*, Goethe changed it for merely acoustic reasons.[9] Obviously, the sequence of fiction and truth is irrelevant—in his sense, truth was relevant only if presented as fiction and all fiction revealed an essential truth more relevant than the incidental truth of history.

Among the innumerable topics dealt with in *Fiction and Truth* we should mention Goethe's very special relation to art—there were times when he thought of becoming a painter rather than a writer. His descriptions of the Dresden art gallery and the Strasbourg cathedral, about which he also wrote a separate essay, are outstanding. More importantly Goethe gives the reader a rather detailed report on the literary scene in Germany during his youth. This has become a rich source of information, as well as offering an insight into Goethe's judgments; and while the judgments are mostly those of the old Goethe writing about the contemporary scene of his youth, the information remains invaluable, since many of his best judgments of the literary scene of that period were undoubtedly formed early.

Included in these discussions are thoughts about the literature of other countries. We encounter views on Italian, French,[10] and English authors, and the rediscovery of Shakespeare in the eighteenth century is clearly reflected in Part III, Book II, where Goethe discusses his English idol on the occasion of Wieland's translation of Shakespeare into German:

Thus Shakespeare, in translation and in the original, in pieces and as a whole, in quotations and excerpts, affected our Strasbourg circle in such a way that, just as there are people with a firm knowledge of the Bible, we acquired gradually a firm knowledge of Shakespeare, imitated in our conversations the virtues and vices of his time with which he had acquainted us, had a lot of fun with his puns, and emulated him by translating them and by our own original whimsicality (494).

It would be easy enough to continue the enumeration of Goethe's topics; his descriptions of landscapes, of people *in* the landscape, of cities, customs, social groups and individuals—the list is endless. The work need not be read in its entirety to be appreciated, yet as a whole it is clearly a great work of art, where detail bears the stamp of the over-all excellence. It is not only an inexhaustible source of information both on Goethe's life and on his times, but it is written with a sure sense of style, of selection, and of pace; it is humorous, ironic, often written with tongue-in-cheek and a very warm understanding of human foibles and failings. If Goethe's mind can be called encyclopedic, it is so in the sense that it embraces so much of life and rarely rejects any of its aspects.

One of the few things Goethe rejects is a tapestry of Jason, Creusa and Medea, hung among others for the reception of the young queen of France, Marie Antoinette (p. 362), in Strasbourg, which he describes as if he considered it an ill omen. If he did not invent the incident, he certainly made the most of it to give to that event the historical depth he could not have foreseen in 1770, but which in retrospect made her visit ominous and overshadowed by an evil future. Here is a typical example of "fiction" in Goethe's sense, adding depth to his narrative by showing the reflection of the queen's life in an object surrounding her.[11] Not a word is said to explain this technique, which is familiar from many of Goethe's prose narratives.

Another way of giving meaning and unity to his story is the insertion of a fairy tale,[12] which is realistically fitted into the biography by the simple fiction that he entered a door in a well-known wall, which he had never observed there before. Goethe thus enters a fairy-tale world which is self-explanatory.

With Goethe's decision to accept the duke's invitation to go to Weimar, the work concludes at the very moment when he definitely enters the adult world of responsibility and of tasks different from the self-imposed work on his poetry. While we have letters and other documentation for the ensuing decade, Goethe wrote no formal work covering this period. His life at the court was not easy, since the duke was very demanding. Goethe also fell in love with Frau von Stein, a married woman older than he, who, in her own way, demanded a large portion of his freedom. At one point the demands of others had to be weighed against those of his own genius, and on September 3, 1786, after ten strenuous, difficult and maturing years, he secretly left the Court to go to Italy:

At 3 AM I sneaked out of Karlsbad (where the Court spent part of the summer), because otherwise they would not have let me depart . . . I threw myself, all alone, into a stagecoach, carrying only a bag and a knapsack and arrived at Zwoda (Czechosolovakia) at 7:30 AM on a lovely, quiet and misty morning.

This is the first paragraph of *The Italian Journey*. Whereas, chronologically, its contents succeed the events described in *Fiction and Truth*, it was not only written earlier, but in an entirely different manner. Using his old notes and diaries Goethe could readily write it, complete with dates, in the present tense and pretend that it was his actual diary. That this is only partially so is obvious from the fully rounded events, tales and observations that give to this work, as they do to *Fiction and Truth*, its artistic unity and significance. The present tense, however, adds a liveliness and immediacy to the experiences which *Fiction and Truth* was never meant to display. Only in its last part did Goethe introduce a few "reports," written in the past tense and in the style of his old age.

The opening paragraph just quoted reveals to the reader the poet's motivation for the trip: to free himself from the shackles of the Weimar court-life and to "find himself," not so much for the sake of a disturbed ego but, above all, for his artistic tasks and ambitions. Goethe was in his late thirties and had started to write a number of works—*Wilhelm Meister, Faust, Iphigenie, Tasso, Egmont*—none of which he had been able to complete to his own satisfaction. He had furthermore started to work in several scientific fields, without contributing anything creative to his studies of nature. He had wasted his time and energy in the service of a minor state and neglected his own superior obligations.

What he could not foresee—although the beginning of the work itself makes it very clear in retrospect—is the impact this trip was to have on his future life. The subtitle "I, too, in Arcadia" indicates what the author found in Italy. His Arcadia has many aspects, only a few of which can be mentioned here. Already in this first diary entry Goethe mentions the sunny weather prevailing on the "fiftieth parallel"—the "southern" parallel on which his home town was situated. Three days later, in Munich, he suggests that fruit is not as good as it should be on the forty-eighth parallel. He counts the parallels because the South is drawing him into its orbit. In Rome, Naples, Sicily, he mentions the glorious sunny days during wintertime. For his eyesight, which was keen and penetrating, the Mediterranean sun produced the quality of light which his favorite painter Claude Lorrain had painted so fervently. His eyes were opened to qualities of light and shade he had never before experienced. But art should not be singled out as the only "product" of the sun, which has a much vaster meaning for Goethe. As we know, in *Faust* it is the central symbol of the World Soul and of wisdom. Goethe does not say this in his *Italian Journey*; but it was at that period of his life that he began to understand to what extent his poetic thought was a symbolic thought and to what degree he used the phenomena of nature as poetic symbols. The sun, understood as a symbol, must have been a powerful experience.

Goethe went to Rome as a student—not as a student of one particular field, but as someone who was open to any kind of new experience and who realized, as he did on the occasion of his first farewell from Rome, that "I did not waste a single moment." Learning, however, takes on an unexpected dimension: "The rebirth, which transforms me from within, continues to work. I thought I would learn here something valuable ("was Rechts"); but that I would have to go back so far in my school years, that I would have to forget what I learned and relearn it completely, that I did not realize" ([December 20, 1786], p. 157).

Almost a year later when some visitors from home "threatened" his voluntary solitude, he avoided seeing them because "The nordic traveler believes that he is coming to Rome to find a supplement to his existence, to fill in some gaps; however, he discovers only gradually and with great uneasiness that he has to change his heart ("Sinn") completely and to start from the beginning" ([Report, October 1787], p. 456).

We witness in the *Italian Journey* the rebirth, i.e., the transformation, of a personality we thought we knew well enough from Goethe's earlier works. A new awareness was created in him, a vast potential of learning new "things," but, above all, of learning to see things in a new manner he had not been able to anticipate. What does the new manner consist of? Histories of literature have always emphasized the fact that the *Italian Journey* meant Goethe's transition from the style of his earlier "Storm and Stress" years to his so-called classical period. While this statement is partially and marginally defensible, it does not in any way represent, in its totality, the new outlook he acquired.

At the beginning of the *Italian Journey*, Goethe was occupied with observations belonging to the natural sciences, biology, botany, and meteorology: "I am engrossed in the impressions of the senses," he writes on the morning of September 11, 1786, "which no book, no painting can offer. What happens is that I take a new interest in the world, test it and try to prove my power of observation." Goethe elaborates on this thought, tries to iron out "the wrinkles of his mind" and feels that it has "a new elasticity." The expansion of the mind, that is attempted in our day with the help of drugs, Goethe found in a trip to Italy, which at his time was a unique experience, mainly enjoyed by painters and writers.

Goethe was also strongly interested in the formation of rocks and clouds. In the interval between his actual trip and its transformation into the *Italian Journey*, he had learned much more about cloud formation; and his lively description of these at the beginning of the book were inserted during the composition of the work.

For the first time Goethe also saw and experienced the sea which had long served him as a poetic symbol without his ever having actually seen it. Quite unclassical is his lively interest in Mount Vesuvius, which he climbed three times in order to be as close to the central crater as he could possibly get. He was as interested in the asphyxiating fumes he breathed as in the glowing lava which he observed in its various stages of hardening (p. 206 and p. 228). In contrast to his friend Tischbein who, as a painter, "is concerned with transforming even the unformed parts of nature such as rocks into humanly beautiful forms" (p. 204), Goethe enjoyed this sign of nature's primitive power and approached it without regard for danger. Upon his return to

Naples (p. 229), watching a beautiful sunset, he meditated on the terrifying contrast which exists in and around the Neapolitan landscape between terror and beauty and came to the conclusion that the strangely indifferent character of the Neapolitans is due to the fact that they feel narrowed in "between God and Satan."

There is another observation to be made. Goethe spent much of his time in Rome in the company of painters who had been settled there for some time. Goethe himself did a number of rather charming sketches, and he liked to look at the Roman landscape (the campagna) with a painter's eye. But whereas, obviously, the themes treated in some of the paintings created by his friends were "classical," i.e., ancient, and their style can be called "classical" because of a certain simplicity of structure and the subdued nature of the colors, these paintings are also full of "romantic" features, such as the ruins in the landscape. To be sure, Goethe, as well as his painter friends, had read Johann Jakob Winckelmann's *Kunst des Altertums* (Art of Antiquity) and had learned to look at the ancient ruins with awe and enthusiasm. But despite the presence of certain classical objects in the paintings, the latter were "modern" in their own opinion and that of their friends. Goethe's ideas on art, as he developed them after his return from Italy, were not so much formed by classical theories of art as by his contacts with his painter friends.[13]

Goethe's literary output of this period will also have to be considered from this point of view of classicism. It is quite true that Goethe tried his hand at classical meters, mainly hexameters and pentameters. He even wrote an "epic," *Herman und Dorothea*,[14] which is more an "idyll," however, than an heroic epic. And he did not use ancient "themes" and myths any more now than he had done as a very young writer. But there *is* a change to be felt in his works of this period when they are compared to his early masterpieces. It is more a change in mood, which is more subdued and less rebellious, than a change in forms or themes. *Iphigenie* offers an example. It is written in Shakespearean blank verse, not in any classical meter. But in its emphasis on resignation and the sacrifice of individual happiness, as well as in the even flow of its lines, and in its strict limitation of the number of characters, it can perhaps be considered more "classical" than *Goetz* or *Egmont*. However, *Iphigenie* resembles Racine's plays much more than those of Sophocles. While there are no scenes in which the *vox populi* is heard, as it had been in Goethe's early plays, there is also no chorus which in Greek drama is the representative of the populace. Moreover, the emphasis is on personal feelings and reactions much more than on the role of an inexorable fate. In short, the ancient gods are replaced by the emotions of the human heart. *Iphigenie* is much closer to Racine, and if it can be called classical, the term must refer to French neo-classicism rather than to the art of the ancients.

There is only one essential feature of ancient poetry which Goethe adopted as a classical stance. It is, in Horace's words, the "Carpe diem," the lively enjoyment of the here and now that Goethe absorbed during his stay in Rome, which is expressed in almost every line of the *Italian Journey*, and which found its literary equivalent in the *Roman Elegies*. The joy of existence, not overshadowed by any metaphysical musings, the immediate, free, and sensuous experience of life's joys and pleasures, is the greatest boon Goethe received from his Italian trip. To feel forms, to see colors, to love without regret, to be unfettered by imposed tasks and obligations, to live an unreflecting life of all the senses —this Goethe considered the greatest heritage from antiquity. Almost every sentence of the *Italian Journey* reflects this carefree attitude, which was strongly supported by the Southern climate and the gay temperament of the Italians.

The term "classical," although in common use by critics who wish to characterize Goethe's literary style after 1787, is unfortunate. It is most fruitfully applied to Goethe's taste in paintings or architecture. Another use of the term, also generally accepted, refers to Schiller's and Goethe's collaboration. It is easy to argue against this usage of "classical," for neither Goethe's nor Schiller's works of the nineties can easily be characterized as classical. There is, however, a classicizing tendency in Schiller's plays of the late nineties, not paralleled in Goethe's works.

IV *Correspondence: Schiller—Goethe*

Ten years Goethe's junior, Friedrich Schiller, had, like his older friend, become famous very early in life with his play *Die Räuber*, which was written in a rather intensified Storm and Stress mood and language. The play was performed at Mannheim in 1781 at a time when, by the simple laws of human growth, Goethe had left his most rebellious years behind. He was over thirty years of age, and minister at the Weimar Court, while Schiller was only twenty-two and still a student. Goethe felt the generation gap acutely, all the more so since he realized the power of Schiller's mind.

It so happened that Schiller came to Weimar in 1787 at a time when Goethe was in Italy. He avidly listened to every report on Goethe by his Weimar friends; and we can see in Schiller's letters to his friend Körner that, whereas he was strongly attracted by the image of the older poet, he also felt alienated. A kind of love-hatred relationship developed which it took Schiller years to overcome.

After his return from Italy, Goethe helped to procure for Schiller a professorship of history at the University of Jena, which belonged to the State of Weimar and where Schiller taught from 1789–99. Goethe was well disposed toward Schiller but remained as reserved as he was to his entire environment. Not until the summer of 1794 did the two men enter into a meaningful conversation. Animated by their exchange of ideas, Schiller sat down to a long letter describing the impression Goethe's mind had made on him. What had impressed him for years and what he had found confirmed in their conversation was Goethe's mental process, entirely his own, of seeking out the natural laws, not by analyzing the phenomena of nature, but by intuitively keeping the wholeness of nature in mind while studying specific phenomena: "From simple organisms you rise, step by step, to the more complex ones, in order to build the most complex phenomenon, man, genetically from the material of the entire structure of nature. By imitating, as it were, nature's own creation, you try to penetrate into her [nature's] hidden technique." (Letter of August 23, 1794.)

The letter is long and complex, but this particular observation seems to have hit the core of Goethe's intellectual, scientific and poetic endeavors. Goethe answered spontaneously and with great warmth, realizing that their conversation meant the beginning of a new epoch of his life; and so he offered Schiller his friendship.

Some weeks before their encounter in Jena, Schiller had asked Goethe to be a contributor and editorial reader to a new cultural magazine he and his friends in Jena planned to publish. Goethe had answered affirmatively. This was obviously the pregnant moment of their relationship in which they became not only understanding friends, but also sensitive collaborators in their stated task of educating the taste and literary judgment of the German public. Thus the personal exchange was immediately bolstered by a common work of major proportions.

Die Horen, as the new magazine was called, became the focal point of their friendship. Many of their literary works of that period were published in it. The two poets could publicly air their ideas on art and literature, and the preparation of each issue became a sounding board on which to test their mutual thoughts. The poetic minds of both men were rejuvenated and fertilized and both had a long spell of great creativity. The correspondence thus serves as a twofold autobiography. Goethe asks Schiller to reveal himself, too, and nothing could have been more gratifying to Schiller than the chance to test his own thoughts against Goethe's response. After having clarified both their differences and their common ground, they sent each other the works they were in the process of writing, in the hope of learning from each other's criticism. It was in the nature of this friendship that Goethe had the more productive and Schiller the better critical mind. If Goethe's works are more frequently discussed than Schiller's, this is not the result of Goethe's otherwise well-known egocentricity. Rather we must understand how much stimulation Schiller received from Goethe's creativity, and Goethe from Schiller's criticism. Whenever Schiller had finished a piece of his own writing he, like Goethe, sent it immediately to his friend for criticism and appraisal. The satisfaction which the reader derives from the letters is due to the even exchange, the complete trust and the mutual stimulation of the two correspondents.

Goethe was unusually ready to contribute to *Die Horen*. He had unpublished material in his desk, above all the *Roman Elegies*. He also sent the Introduction and the first tale of the *Unterhaltungen*. He was then working on *Wilhelm Meister*, the first eight books of which he gradually subjected to his friend's scrutiny. These discussions take up a major part of the correspondence and throw light on the novel. Furthermore, both poets wrote ballads and published their famous and rather mischievous distichs called *Xenien*, in which they lampooned contemporary writers. It is significant that the *Xenien* were not individually signed, but constitute a collective effort. Schiller inspired Goethe to continue his work on *Faust*, and it is in these years that Goethe first conceived of his final plan for the work.

In 1799, Schiller, whose health was failing, moved to Weimar, where both friends worked together to improve the Weimar theater. From this moment on, the correspondence becomes, understandably, less interesting. But even while they lived in the same town and saw each other often, they frequently exchanged manuscripts, accompanied by a note or invited each other by messenger for a meal. The intensive intellectual collaboration of the two friends lasted till shortly before Schiller's death in May, 1805. For the memorial service Goethe wrote the moving poem, "Epilogue to Schiller's *The Bell*," which starts with the words, repeated in the poem several times: "For he was ours." The poem is an apotheosis of the poet, and a reaffirmation of their friendship which outlasted death. It is said that Schiller's name was on Goethe's lips even a few hours before his own death in 1832.

V *Further Autobiographical Material*

After Schiller's death, Goethe no longer recorded his life. As was said earlier, he kept diaries and entertained a vast correspondence. He also had many conversations full of reminiscences with his secretary Eckermann, who wrote them down to preserve Goethe's thoughts for posterity. But it would be an exaggeration to say that these conversations preserve Goethe's own voice. In most instances, we cannot doubt the honesty of Eckermann, who is trustworthy, although pedantic. Sometimes Goethe's words as quoted by Eckermann ring true. But often the lack of an authoritative expression is due to Eckermann's pedantic way of remembering and phrasing Goethe's words. By this time, Goethe had become a legend, and Eckermann treats him with the veneration he feels is due an immortal poet. Surely, much of the

Goethe worship exercised in the nineteenth century is due to his secretary's overawed admiration.

Both as a poet and a man of letters Goethe remained active until his death in 1832. As is befitting a man of his vast intelligence, his thirst for understanding both the world and himself, and his desire to shed light on both, his last words are reported to have been: "More light."

CHAPTER 2

Natural Sciences

I *Nature*

Nature! We are surrounded and enveloped by her—incapable of stepping outside of her and incapable of penetrating deeper into her. Neither asked nor warned, we are received in the cycle of her dance and carried along until we drop, tired, out of her arms.

She creates ever new shapes; what exists has never before existed; what has passed away will not return. Everything is new and yet always the same.

We live in her midst and are foreign to her. She constantly speaks to us, but never reveals her secret to us. We constantly affect her, but have no power over her.[1]

These lines, written in 1783, when Goethe had just[2] started seriously on his own scientific endeavors, provide us with the motivation which drove the poet to a closer study of nature. Many years later (1828), Goethe mentions this short and fragmentary essay on nature in a letter to his friend, Chancellor von Müller and explains to him that, from his later point of view, the attitude toward nature, as it is expressed in the essay, can be judged, to use a grammatical metaphor, only in the "comparative," not in the "superlative." He does not explicitly say so, on this occasion, but it seems clear that there are roughly three stages in the development of Goethe's attitude toward nature.

We can describe the first attitude, expressed mainly in *Werther* and the early poems, as one of an overwhelming emotional response to natural events. The poet loves the rain and the wind; he feels his physical strength restored by nature and establishes an immediate rapport with it, expressed in pantheistic terms. Nature becomes for the poet the great source of poetic inspiration and imagery.

In the second stage, as the letter to von Müller states, Goethe still lacked an intellectual framework which would enable him to penetrate more deeply into the workings of nature—an endeavor which his essay of 1783 seems to consider futile. Only after he developed his concept of metamorphosis did he feel that he had overcome the second stage which he describes as "a kind of pantheism in which an impenetrable, unconditioned, humorous, self-contradictory Being is considered the basis for the phenomena of nature." (XIII, 48.)

Goethe found out, in the years following the essay on nature, that he was indeed capable of penetrating into the secrets of nature by means of scientific studies. Late in his life, when he looked back on these scientific attempts with some satisfaction, he felt that he had made some progress and that others had followed him. Nature appeared a trifle less enigmatic to him now than it did before he took his scientific studies seriously.

Before being able to understand Goethe's urgent desire to occupy his mind with scientific problems, we must take a glance at the situation of the natural sciences during the first half of his life. That this is bound to be an oversimplification hardly needs to be emphasized.

With the help of mathematics, physics and astronomy had been strongly developed over the preceding two hundred years. Their goal was to discover the unalterable laws which govern physical nature. The knowledge of organic matter developed much more slowly. Harvey had discovered the circulation of the blood; Linnaeus had collected and classified plants and animals. The French "philosophers" of the Enlightenment had placed problems of physiology before the public. But the most elementary concepts, such as the cell as the central unit of organic life, was yet undiscovered. Organic chemistry did not exist as a discipline. Psychology as a systematic study of the mind was unheard of, and a psychology based on chemical changes in the body, which Diderot suggested, was anathema to almost everybody.

The philosophic consequences of this rather incomplete scientific image of nature's working were of lasting importance. In his philosophy Descartes, himself a scientist and a mathematician who was deeply interested in physiological problems, had separated the activities of the mind from those of the body in such a fundamental way that it became very difficult for later philosophers to bridge that gap. Some philosophers, convinced that all thinking is entirely subjective, doubted the very existence of the real world, which is obviously largely shaped by the human mind. From a more sociological standpoint, Rousseau had preached that man must return to a state of nature to rid himself of the sociopolitical fetters he had created for himself.

Added to all this must be the prevalent, but weakening, position of religion which held that man is the crown of creation and that the latter was made by God to serve man. For Goethe this was a particularly unacceptable proposition. Whereas he would not deny that man represented the latest stage in the development of nature, he also felt that man belonged to the process of this development, is subordinate to its laws and, basically, part of it. The separation of man from nature, which came about a few decades later through the industrial revolution and man's ensuing desire to dominate and exploit nature, was entirely foreign to Goethe, who felt that nature, i.e., "life," was the essential whole of which man was an intrinsic part.

However, man, in contrast to any other living creature, is simultaneously a part of nature and an observer of it. This puts him in the unique position that he can, at least partly, experience in himself and in his life what it means to be a product of nature. Whereas Goethe made observations on inanimate as well as on animate nature, the latter was particularly important to him, probably for the very reason mentioned here, namely that man himself is an organic part of it. The "life-forces" fascinated him and elicited his curiosity and his diligence.

In his close observation of nature, both animate and inanimate, Goethe was particularly attracted by the eternal change to which all nature is constantly subjected. Almost by definition nothing that exists can last. It will fall apart and will be replaced by some new entity. What is generally known as Goethe's philosophy of "becoming" is his profound experience of change in nature. Nothing static ever exists. Some thinkers find it hard to accept this basic phenomenon of all life—Goethe, however, could, without drowning, swim with the stream of time and change.

It is from this fundamental attitude toward nature that we must understand Goethe's poetic, as well as his scientific, discoveries. For him poetry and science were not disparate activities of man, but simply different means leading to the same end: namely to the discovery and expression of the truth of man's position within the life of nature.

With these preliminary generalizations in mind, we shall look at Goethe's scientific writings from one point of view only: In which ways are his scientific observations essential for our understanding of his literary works; in which ways is it true, as he claims,[3] that science and poetry can be combined and united. Goethe's works show in many different ways that at least his own scientific views are, indeed, incorporated in his poetry, which becomes, as he increases his scientific understanding, almost incomprehensible without a knowledge of the philosophic presuppositions of his scientific concerns.

Goethe's scientific writings are very numerous and embrace a vast variety of topics. They contain a few finished essays which were published during his lifetime and a large number of aphoristic observations, some of which he published, together with his essays, in two volumes called *Schriften zur Morphologie* ("Morphology" [1817–24]). There are also many fine and detailed sketches done in part by himself and in part by others according to his specifications, and a large number of shorter or longer pieces, only part of which were published in the last edition he made of his works.[4] Despite this rich but sometimes sketchy material, there is order and a prevailing sense of unity.

In a postscript to the thirteenth volume of the latest and most completely annotated edition [5] of Goethe's works, the scientist Carl Friedrich von Weizsäcker offers to the layman a lucid and complete presentation of Goethe's main scientific concepts. In many ways I will simply follow Weizsäcker, on whose analysis I can hardly improve. I will, however, keep Goethe's literary productions foremost in mind. In both his late poetry and his *Faust*, his scientific thoughts have found a rather comprehensive expression. It is for this reason that the chapter on science must precede the discussions of his literary works.

II *Form and Change*

Goethe's most elementary experience is the polarity of form and change. Each leaf seems to have its final shape,[6] and yet it has developed out of its bud, will change color, drop down and return to dust. The same tree, a year older and its form slightly enlarged, will produce the same shape of leaf in the following year.

Put in this simple fashion, the truth of this observation may sound trivial, but it is undoubtedly the fundamental problem of life if we view it in nonscientific terms. Goethe, never happy with the abstractions of the physical sciences,[7] needed to find, in his own systematic way, the secrets and mysteries of this essential feature of life.

In his chapter "The Purpose (of the work) is Introduced" (1817) of his *Morphologie* Goethe writes:

> The Germans use the term "Gestalt" for the complexity of the existence of a real being. Through this term they abstract from the changeable character (of the thing) and assume that, by using it, something that belongs together is stated, completed and fixed in its essence.
>
> However, if we observe "Gestalten," particularly organic ones, we find that there does not exist anywhere anything that exists, rests, and is complete, but rather that everything vacillates in constant motion. Therefore our language uses quite correctly the term formation (*Gestaltung*) for what is produced as well as for what is in the state of being produced.
>
> Therefore, if we want to introduce a "morphology," we must not talk about Gestalt. . . .
>
> Everything formed is immediately *trans*formed; and if we want to arrive at a living observation of nature, we must keep ourselves equally flexible and formative, according to the example nature presents to us. (Trunz XIII, 55–56.)

Goethe is saying two things here, one concerning the object observed and another concerning the mind of the observer. Just as the object observed is in a state of constant change, so man, the observer, must allow his mind to be adjusted to this situation by being eternally flexible, open and, therefore, undogmatic. Perhaps it was Goethe's particular genius to be able to follow his own prescription and to keep his mind open and flexible throughout his life. Whereas this attitude may explain his dislike for mathematical formulae, it gives to his poetic works the fluidity and grace that characterize so many of them. He was not only open-minded in his scientific observations but also in his observations of man's behavior, in society as well as in solitude.

The foremost example of an "open" form in Goethe's writings is his *Faust* where the polarity of form and transformation expresses itself in the very structure of the work. Obviously, artistic forms, once they are created, are no longer subject to change unless the author rewrites them. But in *Faust* the fact of change is expressed precisely in its fluid form. To say that Goethe's *Faust* is formless, as some critics have done, is to overlook the essence of the work, which imitates nature in the sense that it manifests, in its form, the very fact of change in its hero.[8]

Goethe's preferred term for transformation was the Greek word "metamorphosis." [9] He first seriously studied plants during his Italian journey and called the essay that resulted from his studies *Versuch, die Metamorphose der Pflanzen zu erklären* (*Attempt to Explain the Metamorphosis of Plants*), 1790. As he relates in a postscript,[10] which he added when he republished the essay in his *Morphologie* (1817), he found it difficult to get a publisher. The public was startled; they had liked the fare he had hitherto put before them and were not ready to accept from him something entirely different. The continuation of the postscript explains [11] how he tried to make his scientific work more acceptable to his friends by writing, in elegy form, a poem addressed to his beloved: *The Metamorphosis of Plants* (1790). It is a lovely poem in the manner of his *Roman Elegies*, in which his more abstract essay comes entirely to life.[12]

The essay itself tries to show how all the stages in the development of a plant can be explained by considering them as metamorphoses of one fundamental type, namely the leaf. He shows how the leaf is contained in the seed, folded up in its tiniest proportions, how flowers, pistils, fruit pods, all seem to be leaves in various stages of transformation. To him, the unity of all plants, their basic principle as it were, is proven by the leaf which is capable of so many transformations. Goethe, as was said before, knew nothing of the existence of cells and believed, therefore, that the metamorphosis of the leaf was indeed the basic principle which assured the continuity of plant life. What he was trying to find was a simple explanation which would show the simple plan according to which nature proceeded when it created the vast variety of plants. Reduction to "unity and continuity" is always the purpose of science, whose basic principle Goethe understood, although botanical science was not far enough developed to make it possible for him to find more satisfactory answers. He himself, however, liked the essay and was amazed and hurt that it found so little echo at the time of its first publication. This situation changed later when younger scientists started where he had left off.

Added to his problems was the fact that Goethe believed in the actual existence of an "original plant" (Urpflanze), i.e., a plant which would contain the pattern for all possible plant developments. While he had originally thought of the *Urpflanze* as an ideal plant, he began to search for it in the real world during his trip to Naples and Sicily. This was an intuitive approach to nature which science, with its reductionist tendency, could not accept.

After his return from Italy when he felt not only misunderstood, but a complete stranger and, as he put it, "fenced in (eingeklemmt) between Heinse's sensuous *Ardinghello* and Schiller's formless *Die Räuber*" he withdrew from his environment. In his essay "Happy Event," published in the *Morphology*, he relates how he tried to avoid a closer acquaintance with Schiller. Then, one day, at a meeting of the Society of Scientists, both authors were present and happened (not quite accidentally on Schiller's part) to leave together. On this occasion, Schiller invited Goethe to his house, and, after listening carefully to Goethe's exposition of the "symbolic plant," said to Goethe, shaking his head: "This is no experience, it is an idea"—undercutting Goethe where he was most vulnerable. After a moment's pause, however, Goethe, understanding the point which Schiller was making, answered: "I should be very glad to have ideas without knowing it and even seeing them with my eyes."

Out of this incident arose the friendship discussed above. They had hit the essence of their different ways of thinking: Schiller, the pupil of Kant, emphasized the structure of the mind, i.e., he felt that the human mind was constituted in such a way as to shape its experiences. Goethe, the realist, (as he calls himself in that essay) felt that experience of reality was the datum out of which man creates his inner world. The inquiry into the struggle between object and subject, which can never be completely settled, he says in his essay (p. 23), was, nevertheless, the cause of his lasting bond with Schiller.

II *Unity and Continuity in Nature*

What made his insight into the metamorphosis of the leaf so important to Goethe was his strong conviction that nature does not proceed in leaps, but rather in a steady development. This is the fundamental presupposition for any idea of evolution, and in this respect Goethe came close to Darwin's ideas. The concepts of perpetual change, metamorphosis and strict continuity are essential for any understanding of man as "part of nature." How disturbing they became in Darwin's formulation is a well-known fact of history.

We have an example of Goethe's sense of the continuity of nature in his famous poem "Gingo Biloba" from the *West-Eastern Divan*. Goethe considered the Ginkho tree as being transitional between coniferous and deciduous trees because of the arrangement of its branches as well as the veins in each leaf. While its "leaves" look like a leaf, their veins run in a parallel fashion, as they do in needles. That Goethe used the phenomenon as a symbol for his relationship to the beloved is typical of the way in which he used his scientific observations in his poetry.

Perhaps more important for the problem of continuity in Nature is Goethe's discovery of the intermaxillary bone, a bone well developed in many animals but, so scientists thought, non-existent in man. This fact had been used as one of the arguments for the essential difference between man and animal. Goethe discovered, in 1786,[13] that there was a clear relic of this bone in the human skull, thereby refuting the idea of the essential difference between man and animal. One important argument of the scientific opposition to the idea of evolution was thus removed.

III *Polarity and Growth*

Polarity is one of Goethe's key terms, indicating the manner in which nature proceeds in its perpetual development and change. What he calls polarity is fairly similar to Hegel's concept of dialectics. To be sure, Goethe's thinking does not proceed in terms of thesis, antithesis and synthesis but, while not arriving at a synthesis, he sees the opposing forces of nature as the only means by which any development can take place. Examples of polarities abound in nature: life and death, day and night, summer and winter (or hot and cold), inhaling and exhaling are only a few characteristic examples. Without polarity there would be no life.

However, Goethe was not satisfied with postulating polarities.

While they provide the manner in which life proceeds, they do not provide explanations. At this point in his thinking (and I have systematized Goethe's thought more than he ever would have liked it to be done) Goethe introduced his basic philosophic (or perhaps better religious) faith. In neoplatonic terms, with which he had become acquainted very early in his life, he considered the whole of material existence as the emanation of a world-soul whose essence consists of its drive to be creative. When the world-soul stirs, as it must according to its very nature, it creates and recreates. Thus "matter" is its created product. Simultaneously, however, the world-soul is not separated from its creation, but is rather, itself, part of it by being manifested in it. The world-soul manifests itself in matter—this is its act of creation. However, since it is spirit, it is also more than its manifestations which are never pure spirit. Thus, in an eternal cycle, all creation desires to go back to its original, nonmaterial origin. Ultimately, therefore, Goethe's concept of change, development, and metamorphosis, which he observed so well as a natural phenomenon, is rooted in his belief in a living world-soul which manifests itself in life while simultaneously striving to withdraw from life and become pure spirit again.

Steigerung (meaning both growth and improvement), means for Goethe the transformation of living things into a more spiritual state of existence. It exists in nature as well as in man and is nothing but a certain restlessness of all created things, which, having never quite lost contact with their spiritual origin, tend to strive to regain this spirituality. *Faust* is the work that most consistently expresses this innate desire for *Steigerung*.[14]

All of this, as was said above, can be considered as an outdated metaphysical stance. However, what fascinated Goethe is the fact that the specific phenomena he actually studied confirmed his earlier vague metaphysical concepts. The perpetual movement and change he found the most striking feature of everything existing was, to him, a proof of the metaphysical truth so deeply ingrained in him. He overcame Descartes's separation of body and mind by considering both as manifestations of the world-soul in different degrees of *Steigerung*. And while this might be considered a regression from the point of view of the development of philosophy, it is simultaneously a great step forward in the direction of a biological understanding of man. While Goethe did not quite state that mind may have developed out of body, he anticipates this thought by his observations on evolution and his acceptance of polarity and growth, because the latter—not used as a moral term—expresses the progression in the animal world from the lower to the higher species. While modern scientists cannot accept the myth of the world-soul —very dear to Goethe's poetic thinking—they find him in many ways an astonishingly modern and advanced scientific thinker.

IV *Theory of Colors*

Between 1790 and 1810, i.e., the date of publication of his *Theory of Colors*, Goethe observed colors, made experiments and gave a great deal of thought and energy to optics. Here we are not interested in the details of his findings, which are often fascinating and based on interesting observations. We can only briefly discuss the reasons for his continued interest and curiosity and their philosophic basis. Goethe contradicted Newton's theory that colors are a result of the refraction of light because, for him, a purely mathematical explanation was unsatisfactory. Instead, his *Theory of Color* starts with an extensive chapter on the physiological aspects of color, which he entitles "Physiological Colors." Here he discusses all manners of situations in which the eye creates its own color-scheme which is nowhere to be found in the reality of the objects, but is exclusively the product of the onlooker. We have all experienced such phenomena without insisting on collecting and systematizing them as Goethe did so successfully.

The physiological colors form the first chapter of Part One of the *Theory of Color*, called "Didactic Part." Two further chapters belong to this *Didaktischer Teil*: "Physical Colors" and "Chemical Colors." Omitting here the physical colors, which Goethe describes as very fugitive and not belonging to the essence of the object on which they appear, we will turn to the chemical colors which are, to a certain extent, inherent in the chemical composition of an object, or, at least, the chemical process produces *in* the object the appearance of colors.[15]

This is an overly condensed presentation of Goethe's attempt to separate in his mind the components needed to describe the phenomenon "color." It is obvious, even from such a brief overview, that Goethe's interest went far beyond Newton's refraction of the light-ray. From Newton's scientific-mathematical vantage point, which searches for valid natural laws in an objective world, Goethe seemed to be quite mistaken. And scientists have always shaken their heads about Goethe's erroneous interpretation. But Goethe had valid reasons for his attitude. He himself had observed the phenomenon of colors in Italy, where the Southern light produces much stronger colors than the dimmer light in Germany allows. On the same occasion, he had also been in the company of painters who had been strongly attracted precisely by the Southern colors. This type of color problem is of no interest to the scientist, but is of foremost interest to the artist. Goethe tried to tackle the phenomenon of color from an aesthetic point of view.

Aesthetic theories of color were in their infancy. Less than one hundred years earlier, Shaftesbury had considered himself to be very bold when he spoke of paintings at all. Goethe went far beyond Shaftesbury. He made some startling discoveries that were entirely new at his time and elaborated on many years later by the Impressionists. In the first place, the idea that art must rely on sense impressions rather than on ideas and pictorial organization was a new one. The subjective aspect of color impressions made on the senses fascinated him. Thus he noted at one point: "It is blasphemy to say that there is such a thing as an optical delusion." This means that, when the painter has an optical color impression, he is entitled to reproduce it in his painting regardless of what physics thinks the correct color ought to be. The impressionists operated precisely on this level of understanding of sense impressions, which may be subjective but are nonetheless. true. Even Picasso was unwittingly following Goethe's subjective color scheme when he painted a blue or pink lady.

Goethe goes one step further, however: He carefully observed the colors in the shadow thrown by an object. Monet, to give just one example, painted precisely the colors of shadows and studied, as Goethe had done, the effect of light, or the lack of it, on colored surfaces. Goethe opened up an entire realm of aesthetic experiment and experience, understood and followed only decades later.[16]

The last section (VI) of the Didactic Part is called "The Sensuous-Ethical Effect of Color." In it, Goethe attributes certain

[47]

effects on man of certain colors—a phenomenon we all know for example from decorating a room. He speaks of cheerful or warm or cold colors, etc., and ends with a brief excursus on the "allegoric, symbolic, mystic use of color" (p. 520) which is only a logical sequence of describing colors as having what we might call "meaning." If blue, e.g., has an effect of coolness, it logically can be used in art and literature as a symbol of coolness. This is very old lore, put together by Goethe systematically as constituting one of the many aspects of color.

Goethe, who disliked abstractions and steered away from apparatus, substituted for these scientific tools his own lively experience of color. Being endowed with a very acute sense of sight and a tolerable artistic talent, he felt the need to systematize his experiences and make them appear more objective than can reasonably be expected. The *Farbenlehre* reads like an extended record of optical experiences from which any writer or painter can choose the material appropriate to his needs. It did not occur to Goethe to write a systematic treatise on aesthetics for which he had all the material in his hand. He followed his usual scientific practice of collecting observations systematically and in great quantities without ever wishing to derive from them the abstract laws for which the true scientist would be searching. The colorful world was much too rich and varied for his discerning eye ever to yield to philosophic or scientific abstraction. His theory of colors was rudimentary, restricted to a collection of visual detail. But since these details are seen with an artist's eye, it provides material for an aesthetic theory, which its author would never have wished to write. For us, its importance lies in the field of aesthetics, but in this field it is startlingly modern, progressive and original.

V *Other Scientific Observations*

To Goethe's observations on plant growth and color impressions we could add any number of his scientific enterprises. I will add only two examples which clearly show how Goethe derived some of his poetic techniques from his scientific observations. The first one is not his own discovery. Luke Howard had written his work on cloud formation in 1805,[17] but Goethe had read it only ten years later. In his introduction to a biography of Howard's life, which the author sent to him upon Goethe's request, Goethe writes: "How desirable the formation of the formless, the metamorphosis of the unlimited according to laws must have been to me follows from my entire endeavor in science and art." (XIII, 304)

Goethe does not exaggerate. His life's work can be summarized as a "formation of the formless," and his real tendency was to overcome chaos by transforming it into something that has its own laws. If we add to this his love of water in its varying shapes and appearances,[18] we can readily understand Goethe's fascination.

Not only did Goethe write a famous sequence of poems dedicated to Howard, but he used Howard's useful classifications of cloud formations in many of his prose-works, as well as in *Faust*, with symbolic reference to Howard's terms. What the scientist Howard avoided, i.e., a symbolic application of his scheme to human life, the poet Goethe uses with delight. Nothing shows more abundantly than Goethe's poetic usage of cloud formations the extent to which he could meaningfully combine scientific and poetic thinking without doing damage to either. He does not deviate from Howard's scientific truth, but he finds in it a symbolic value which the scientist could not have foreseen.

In a similar way, Goethe used a certain optical phenomenon, called entoptic colors, as a model for the structure of his own literary productions. Entoptic colors occur if a glass cube which is, in quick succession, heated and cooled is reflected in two parallel mirrors. In these mirrors one sees repeatedly reflected a black and white cross surrounded by beautiful colors. As one changes the angles of the mirrors, the cross changes into dots, but the colors remain. In his *Theory of Colors* Goethe wrote about his various experiments in Entoptics.

In an essay called "Wiederholte Spiegelungen" ("Repeated Mirror Reflections," 1823), Goethe relates this natural phenomenon to the memory of man. As these mirror reflections become stronger and more beautiful through their repeated appearance, so the psychological reflections, caused by man's repeated recall of a person or situation, strengthen the remembered image and make it, as time goes by, ever more lovely. In this essay Goethe finds beautiful words for the psychological phenomenon that so closely resembles the scientific observations he had made in Entoptics.

Other examples could easily be added. In Goethe's mind there vas no gap between what nature produces and what man, in is daily life, produces or experiences. For him there were no two cultures," there was rather a sense of truth which revealed tself in nature as well as in the life of man. Either one was a mbol of the other.

CHAPTER 3

Poetry

I *Introduction*

IF Goethe had not said, in *Dichtung und Wahrheit*, that his poems were "fragments of one large confession," Goethe scholars might have discovered much earlier that what Goethe must have meant when he made the statement was different from what his enthusiastic readers understood when they interpreted it. No author can write anything but a confession, because his thinking, feeling, imagining, the conscious and unconscious content of his creative mind, naturally enter into his every word and sentence. Where the readers of Goethe's works were mistaken was in their literal interpretation of his statement. They searched in his poems for biographical detail rather than poetic achievement. And while it is, of course, true that some of Goethe's many loves are recognizable in his poems, the same can be said of most great poets. In fact, it is a compliment to Goethe's poetic genius that his love poems, with rare exceptions, do not require any biographical knowledge for their understanding. They do, however, require detailed and careful interpretation because they are complex and often very difficult to analyze. A discussion of Goethe's lyrical poetry should, therefore, proceed from a consideration of its formal elements.[1]

A poet as highly educated and as widely read as Goethe must be expected to work with both traditional and original forms. This distinction has, at times, been made the criterion for the quality of Goethe's lyric poetry. Friedrich Gundolf, in his *Goethe*,[2] has a different term for this same distinction. He sorts out Goethe's poetry according to the experience behind the poem, which, in Gundolf's view, can either be a personal, "original" experience or one produced by one's reading and education. This distinction, it seems to me, is invalid because both types of experience are almost always mixed in his poetry and do not require any essential choice of him. Some of Goethe's traditional forms may be highly original in content and language, and some of his "original" forms are utterly trivial. Whereas, on the one hand, Goethe was a great innovator of poetic forms, he was also a very well-read man who delighted in giving traditional forms a new poetic life. He succeeded equally well in both endeavors.

There is almost no traditional poetic form, either ancient or "modern" in its widest sense, which Goethe did not apply at one time or another in his long career as a writer of poetry. Hexameters, the elegiac meter, blank verse, "Knittelverse," [3] Alexandrines, *ottaverime* and other rhythms and stanzas appear at certain points in his work, being used for specific purposes and rejected whenever considered useless. On the other hand, there exists an equal wealth of original forms and meters. From his earliest poetic attempts to his late, mature poems, Goethe has not only an unerring instinct for poetic expression, but a mastery of language, imagery, and sound, as well as of meters, rhythms and rhymes which makes him indeed the "richest" poet of the German language; the extent to which he contributed to the creation of the modern German poetic idiom, both in poetry and prose, can hardly be overstated.

Already in his teens Goethe abandoned the Alexandrine and turned to shorter iambic verse as the more appropriate Germanic meter.[4] However, despite this correct insight, which was just beginning to be common knowledge on the German literary scene, his early poems have a strangely conventional flavor; they sound like a talented student's more or less imitative endeavors. It is not only a question of such conventional expressions as "the breeze of Zephyr" or similar "anacreontic" devices, nor is it the slightly sugary taste of his somewhat lewd and thoroughly artificial love-songs, but the thoughts and images are equally uninspired. The only notable exceptions are three odes to a friend, whom he tries to console for having lost his position. They contain a healthy degree of genuine rebellion. For the first time we hear the author's own voice.

I am dwelling on this lack of originality because it shows what a long way an eighteenth-century author had to go before he could arrive at that expression of his own "genius," which was to be the mark of Goethe's early successes. During the course of his long life, Goethe was often called upon to write poems for special public occasions. And whenever such an occasion arose, he would fall back—more consciously than in his late teens—on such conventional poetry as must have pleased his contemporaries far better than his profounder and often uncanny poetic insights. Perhaps eighteenth-century poetic conventions, of which there were many, served the poet well in later years as a kind of mimicry behind which the lonely genius could hide at times.

I will forgo a discussion of the poems written during his student days at Strasbourg, in which one can, for the first time, discern a poetic awakening, although "Zephyr" still blows and love-songs still come all too easily. In 1771 we notice a sudden and radical breakthrough of Goethe's own voice in the first of his great "Pindaric" odes, "Wanderers Sturmlied" (Wanderer's Storm-Song).[5] From that time on, and for the next fifteen years, Goethe was drawn to this particular form and wrote most of his greatest poems in it. While he honestly intended to imitate Pindar's Odes with their irregular rhythms, he was actually creating something entirely new: free verse and free rhythms, a kind of poetry for which, a hundred years later, the French Symbolists were searching and even fighting, and which has invaded contemporary poetry only very recently. Goethe was not attempting to create a new genre—nor could he completely foresee the effect the new form would have on his own future productions. With the insights he had won during his stay at Strasbourg, he felt the urgent need to free himself from bonds of conventions, in everyday life as well as in his poetic expression. The results are some of the most original poems written in the German language.

II *The Pindaric Odes*

Goethe's odes consist of stanzas with an irregular number of lines, and lines with an irregular meter. There is no rhyme, but an incisive rhythm, different from line to line and from stanza to stanza, but kept under control by certain formal devices. Not only is each stanza held together by a distinct unity of thought, often expressed in a single sentence, but the individual stanzas are interconnected by a repetition or near-repetition of their first lines. Thus, the first lines of the first four stanzas of "Wanderer's Storm-Song" are almost identical: "Whom you, Genius, do not desert. . . ." Repetition or near-repetition of lines occur also frequently within one stanza, to the point where the reader anticipates such repetitions.[6] Sometimes, the connecting link between two lines or stanzas is formed by a single significant word (e.g., "Wärme" in "Wanderer's Sturmlied"). Both stanzas and individual lines are also richly interconnected by assonances and alliterations which, again, can almost be anticipated by the reader. One of the most remarkable features of these poems is the forceful placing of words and phrases within the rhythm. As a result, certain words or phrases seem "naturally" accented when, actually, these effects betray a high degree of artistic craft. In "Prometheus" e.g., one stanza starts with the simple phrase "Who helped me"—a sentence to which the answer is: "Not the gods, but I myself." Against expectation, the accent in the German text is on "who," not on "helped." It is indeed a central phrase, simple though it sounds. Its directness functions as a kind of title for this stanza and, therefore, stands out in the ear of the reader as a monumental motif. A similar role is assigned to the first lines in each stanza of this particular poem.

What makes these poems distinctive, however, is the creation of a symbolic mythical figure around which the poem is arranged (Prometheus, Ganymed, Mohamet, etc.). The poet projects his own thoughts and experiences onto his hero, objectifying them and manipulating them as do all truly modern poets who use ancient myths in such a way as to create truly "modern" figures.

The three main mythical poems by Goethe are "Mahomets Gesang" ("Mohamet's Song") "Ganymed," and "Prometheus." The first, conceived as part of an unfinished play, was, in the original version, sung by two characters.[7] The title is our only indication that Mohamet is its subject. In this ode, the mythical, rather than the historical, hero is symbolized by a river whose course is described, as it runs from its source to the ocean, in a series of river images which, in turn, symbolize the history not only of a great leader of men, but also that of individual man or all mankind. The rapid or slow flow of the water, its trip toward the ocean, the eternal father, from whence the clouds rise which, in turn, will refeed the source of the river, was one of Goethe's most perfect images of his conception of life. For him, life was a stream in constant motion which issues from a source, the World-Soul, and flows into the ocean, the same World-Soul, which restores its power and makes it start again at its source in an eternal circular movement.

The power of the over-all metaphor is great. Above the clouds in the mountains "he (i.e., the river) was nursed by kindly spirits." His first appearance is dance-like, and while his motion is, by the necessity of the life-cycle, downward, his first jubilant outcry goes up toward Heaven. After the "brother-springs" have joined him, he creates flowers and meadows, but their loving eyes cannot stop his ineluctable course. In the plains he is joined by his "brother-streams" who would be lost without his greater power. And now his real task begins: he names countries, creates cities, towers, marble-houses—and leaves them all behind. Like Atlas he carries "cedar-houses," i.e., boats, and their sails point again to Heaven. And, streaming with joy, he carries his brothers and children to the heart and the open arms of the creator.

This short paraphrase does not do justice to the images whose immediate metaphorical power hits the reader forcefully. More important even than the rich imagery are the free rhythms. Each line begins with an accented syllable, which is never followed by more than one unaccented one. It is a strict trochaic meter, with an uneven number of trochae in each line. There are a few internal rhymes and many assonances. The main poetic device is the repetition of words and lines, which produces the feeling of great urgency. As is possible in German, nouns are skillfully placed before or after the verb, and sometimes manipulated in such a way that one noun stands at the end of a clause and another, seemingly belonging to the preceding verb, suddenly reveals itself as the subject of a new verb (19–20, 57–58). Articles are omitted, and so are the words "as" and "like." Compound nouns and adjectives abound, many of them of Goethe's own creation. Despite its length, the poem has a great density. While the mythical meaning is never lost sight of, the metaphor is consistently carried through without ever turning into what Goethe himself would call allegory.[8] One might say that one myth, that of Mahomet, is presented in terms of another myth, that of the flowing river. The two are one, and the reader experiences them as one without ever losing sight of the double meaning.

By contrast to this very objective myth, the "Ganymed" poem expresses a more personal yearning for a reunion with the world-soul, a youthful abandonment of the ego in a loving embrace of the godhead. Compared to the mature man represented in Mohamet's river-image, Ganymed would youthfully venture on the shortest way from man to God, for which Faust yearns in vain, as will be seen later. At dawn, Ganymed addresses Spring as "Beloved," thus anticipating the mood of the entire poem, which represents a blend of sexual and mystical longing. And as it ends with the words "all-loving father," Ganymed is carried upward in the "womb" of the clouds, and the embrace of father and child is both active and passive (embracing, embraced). Goethe often toys with the exchangeability of the sexes.

Quite different from the attitude of the poems just discussed is the poem "Prometheus," which was written at the time when Goethe was also trying to write a play on the same myth. A large fragment of the play is preserved, but the poem constitutes an independent monologue, which is one of Goethe's most rebellious expressions. It is a radical rejection of the gods, not because they don't exist, but because their existence has no bearing on man's life. Only children and beggars hopefully expect their help, which will not be forthcoming. Prometheus became a man by the work of "almighty Time" and "eternal Fate," the gods' masters as well as his own. And the poem ends with the most self-assertive stanza Goethe ever wrote:

> Here I sit forming man
> after my own image
> a family like me
> to suffer, to cry
> to enjoy and be happy
> and not to honor you
> as I do.

The language of the poem is truly blasphemous. Goethe always used biblical language and loved it, but other than in *Faust* he never used it with such scathing intent. There is nothing sentimental in this Prometheus—an eighteenth-century rebel figure of great power who stands on his own ground and despises the gods.

If we compare the three odes, three totally different attitudes emerge. While they are all, in some way, expressions of the idea of genius, each figure represents a very different aspect of the phenomenon. Mohamet is powerful only because his life unfolds within the cosmic life cycle. There is, on the one hand, no rebellion and, on the other, no mystic union in the poem. Ganymed, both the lover and the beloved, yearns for the union with the World-Soul, unconscious of the existing life-cycle and, therefore, unwilling to participate in it. And Prometheus, although a creator, does not create within the life-cycle, but unlike Mahomet, rebelliously outside of it.

It seems clear from this brief discussion of the content and attitude of the three poems that a biographical interpretation would run into the difficulty (unwarranted if we omit biographical references) of deciding where the young poet stood with regard to the fundamental questions of man and his place in the world. Goethe, however, was a considerably more objective poet than he is often given credit for being, and carried his mythological poems through with the internal consistency which the subject required.

Another group of odes are those whose central figure is a wanderer. Goethe liked to present himself in this disguise, which we find, throughout his life, used as an image of himself, even at a time when he was well settled in Weimar.[9] The Wanderer poems start with the "Storm-Song" mentioned earlier. Inspired by a walk in the rain, the poet muses about this poetic inspiration, addressing ancient gods and muses, as well as ancient poets. Only Pindar, he realizes, was capable of writing such storm-inspired poetry, and the poet tries to rival him. But the poem, being also the song of a man caught in the rain, ends comically with a prayer that he may reach his dry cabin.

More than any other hymn, the poem is characterized by compound words [10] and very complex sentence structures. It shifts with great ease from one god, and one poet, to another, from the ancient poetic world to the present, very prosaic situation. Their common bond is the *furor poeticus*, the almost violent poetic inspiration. For the first time, Goethe fully experienced what his Storm and Stress contemporaries called genius—a concept this poem helped considerably to establish.

"An Schwager Kronos" (To Coachman Kronos) is another journey, taking place in a coach going up and down mountains, and ending, comically, in an inn.[11] What is actually symbolized by the coachtrip is man's journey through life. The poem ends in the evening when the coach rattles and the old man who is undertaking the journey travels directly downhill toward Hades —where the innkeeper will gladly receive him. This ending is a change Goethe made when he prepared the first edition of his Works in 1789. In the original version, the old man is received in Hades by the "powerful ones"—presumably the ancient poets who accept him in their midst. While this may be the more forceful version, the self-irony of the later version shows a growing degree of self-awareness, perhaps more acceptable to us than the arrogant self-assurance of the first one.

The next of the wanderer odes is considerably less self-assured. It is called "Harz-Mountain Trip in Winter." Goethe, who was already in Weimar at this time (1777), undertook a real trip on horseback to the Harz Mountains, partly in order to inspect the mines, partly to meet a young man (Plessing) who had written him some despairing letters. In the poem, these biographical facts are barely hinted at, and the unknowing reader might easily identify the unhappy poet in the poem, who disappears in the woods, with the author of the ode. That this is not so, however, is evident from the opening stanza where the ode is compared to a vulture who, resting on the heavy morning clouds, searches for his prey. The prey of the poem is the unhappy person who "drank hatred of men from the fullness of love." And the author prays to the Father of Love to pour love into the heart of the unfortunate young man.

The style of the odes—the fullness of images, the shortened syntax, the existence of a god and the immediacy of surrounding nature, is entirely preserved in this poem. But the tone has changed, the "I" has almost completely disappeared, and the concern of the poem is the other, invisible person. The experience of the journey to the top of the snowy mountain is still exhilarating, and it is in motion alone that nature is revealed to the poet. But his heart and his prayer are with and for the other man.

III *The Weimar Poems*

During the first ten years of his stay in Weimar Goethe's style underwent great changes, conditioned partly by his growing maturity and his strongly developing sense of responsibility, which are not manifest in the exuberance of the early hymns. And it was influenced partly by his unfulfilled love of Charlotte von Stein, who, his senior by seven years and married, became a demanding presence in his life. One of his most beautiful love-poems ("Why did you give us the deep glances . . .") was found after Goethe's death among the one thousand seven hundred letters and notes addressed to Charlotte von Stein.[12]

In these years, Goethe composed more odes in the form of the earlier ones, unrhymed, with an uneven number of lines per stanza, and an uneven meter in the lines. They are, in their own way, as beautiful as the earlier hymns, but very different in tone, meaning and imagery. They do not have a central figure informing the poem. Instead, they have a central idea that expresses a general truth about man and is clothed in one or several rich images. Their tone is much more quiet, even resigned, and the ideas have a moral bent—something totally absent from the earlier poems. The poet's youthful rebellion is over, and he assesses man's role on this earth. Myth, however, is present, although somewhat less all-embracing. It is used metaphorically rather than as a total symbol, and the images are more clearly images, rather than symbolic structures.

An outstanding example is the "Gesang der Geister über den Wassern" (*Song of the Spirits Above the Waters*) (1779) which presents the reader with the same water cycle which had been so jubilantly explored in "Mohamet's Song." It is not only different in mood, being much more pessimistic, resigned and subdued, but it also takes the water-cycle image as a metaphor, rather than a symbol, and speaks more immediately about man's soul and fate:

> Des Menschen Seele
> Gleicht dem Wasser:
> Vom Himmel kommt es,
> Zum Himmel steigt es,
> Und wieder nieder
> Zur Erde muss es,
> Ewig wechselnd.
>
> Man's Soul
> Resembles water,
> It comes from Heaven,
> Rises to Heaven,
> And must go down again
> Toward the Earth,
> Eternally changing.

Apart from this fact, Goethe's poetic means have not greatly changed. The first lines of the irregular stanzas retain their monumental simplicity, expressing the theme of each stanza in the shortest and clearest way possible. Vowels and consonants appear in a rich profusion of assonances and alliterations. Each stanza has its own tonality. The i-sounds of the first one indicate the eternal cycle, the rising and falling of the water and the human soul. In the third stanza, *u* becomes the dominant sound, as cliffs oppose the water's downward course. The same u-sounds are repeated in the fifth stanza, as the wind stirs the water's gentle waves to destruction. And the whole image is pulled together in the last stanza, as the poet returns to the idea of the first line of the poem and consciously compares man's soul with the water, and his fate with the wind.

In comparison with the earlier poems, where the identification of the symbol and the thing symbolized (namely, man in his various attitudes) is complete, the later hymns are more mature. The pantheistic exuberance gives way to a greater reflectiveness and a distance between the subject-matter and the metaphor or, as in this instance, between man and nature.

Man's role and participation in nature is one of the great themes that run through Goethe's work. For the young poet, Nature was an object of delight and, in his pantheistic moments, the manifestation of the World-Soul of which he attempted to become a part. In his mature years, nature, mainly in the biological sense, became the object of his scientific research. But in either phase it remained above all, a source of poetic inspiration furnishing the poet with images and a symbolic framework. In fact, Goethe's entire literary production draws on nature, and few are the images that are not connected with it.

Man's role in nature is a permanent concern of the poet and finds many varied expressions. While we cannot expect any serious disharmony between man and nature in his works, we also (as in the present poem) no longer find that youthful and complete identification of the two elementary phenomena, nature and man, which preoccupied Goethe's earlier thinking. The poetic phenomenon of an increased distance between the symbol and the object symbolized indicates, simultaneously, the greater distance the poet felt existed between man and his natural environment. Whether at this particular moment of his life he was fully aware of his new philosophic attitude is irrelevant. The fact remains that the poem discussed here clearly and poetically expresses such a newly won attitude.

The next ode is a lovely poem on Imagination, daughter of Zeus and wife of the poet. The third, "Grenzen der Menschheit" (Limits of Mankind), starts with the "old, holy father" who sows lightning over the earth. But this is only an effective introductory gesture; in the rest of the poem, the divine is mentioned only as "gods" and is compared with "man," the true subject of the piece. The gods may be able to encompass the entire Chain of Being in one glance, but man is confined to observing only one link in the chain and cannot see beyond. Almost in answer to this thought about the limitation of man in time and space, the next poem, "Das Göttliche" (The Divine), emphasizes the moral power bestowed on man who can "give duration to this short moment" by being able to distinguish between good and evil. But, more than that, man's moral behavior should serve as an example and image which enables us to believe in the gods—who, as in "Prometheus," do not influence man to do good. Clearly, man is the center of the poet's concern, and the gods are pushed to the margin of man's existence on earth. They may have powers over nature, but man is free to make his own moral choices.

The preceding discussion of the philosophic position of the odes does no justice to their poetic quality. Goethe was by now in complete mastery of his poetic idiom, and each of these odes, as well as many of the lyrical poems written during the same period, can be said to be perfect. The language and the rhythms have become smoother, and the rush of the earlier odes has subsided and given way to a more balanced harmony. The ideas, as discussed above, are sparse and concise, and nothing in the poems remains hidden and obscure. The youthful rebel has been tamed, but the flow of his poetry was not damaged by the taming which Goethe owed, in part, to Charlotte von Stein. Ultimately, he himself wanted to be tamed—it was a process of maturing he much needed, if he was not to continue writing in a youthful style no longer congenial with his age. What he may have lost in spontaneous expression he gained in depth of insight and verbal dexterity.

The poem, "Warum gabst du uns die tiefen Blicke" (Why Did You Give Us the Deep Glances), mentioned above, indicates this direction in his poetic development most clearly. The poem retains, in part, the uneven number of lines per stanza of the odes; but perhaps it would be better described as having regular eight-line stanzas, with the exception of the second, much longer one. It is further distinguished from the odes by having regular alternating rhymes, the first and third lines being, throughout, endowed with feminine rhymes,[13] the second and fourth, on the other hand, having masculine rhymes. The lines have five trochaic feet. In other words, Goethe here created one of his own favorite stanzas which he used to great advantage in his later poems. However, he never published this particular poem in his collections of poetry, and did not even own a copy of it.

The poem is written against a background of faith in the transmigration of the soul. However, it is not the poet's soul which is subject to transmigration, but rather the relationship to the beloved, which remains unchanged in the past, the present and the future. He calls it a true relationship (wahr Verhältnis) and compares it to most human relationships, which are "dumpf" (obtuse) and in which the partners never know each other. Repeatedly, he envies those relationships which are not burdened by the "deep glances" into the future or the memories of times past.

The myth of transmigration is the unifying bond between past, present and future. It is carried through with complete consistency: "Ahndung" (premonition) refers to the future, "Erinnerung" (memory) to the past. The tenses vary accordingly, but the future tense is absent, since the future is seen only through the premonition of the present. The poem moves from this premonition, through the comparison with the unknowing "others," to an extensive memory of the past when the beloved was "my sister or my wife." And it ends in the painful present, where the only happiness is the faith that the relationship is unchangeable.

Much has been said about the dim memory in which the distinction between sister and wife is blurred. No doubt, Goethe was very fond of his own sister, and a slight tendency toward incest may easily be spotted here and in other parts of Goethe's works. As we shall see, Goethe also was attracted to hermaphrodites, or perhaps rather to the stage of adolescence where a boy might develop into either of the sexes. But just as this attraction is only marginally connected with homosexuality, so the relationship to his sister has little connection with incest. Goethe was more perceptive than most of his contemporaries and discovered in himself sexual tendencies which most people carefully repress. However, this poem is very far removed from sexuality, perhaps even too far for his own good. The memory's dimness rather indicates a closeness to the beloved, to the point where he feels understood by her as by a sister. The emphasis is on the amazing understanding the beloved has for him, as if she had known him from childhood on, as only a sister can know a man. Whether this particular passage determined Goethe against publication, we do not know. From any point of view, it is an unconventional statement which produces the effect of a profound insight, a "deep glance," into a relationship simultaneously profound and frustrating.

Another of the mysterious and profound poems of this period is called "An den Mond" (To the Moon). There are two very different versions of the poem. The second, more complete one will be discussed here.[14]

The poem is addressed to the moon and returns, in the end, to the nightly scene. But the landscape on which the moonlight quietly rests is that of the human heart, and the moon is compared to a compassionate friend. The human and the natural scene are intimately interwoven. In the third stanza, the poet "wanders" alone between happiness and misery, and in the fourth stanza, without transition, the river along which he wanders becomes the very image of this wandering man. As man moves between happiness and misery, so the river flows between winter and spring. The present scene is thus momentarily abandoned for a glance at the future and the past. And yet, none of these subtle changes gives the reader the impression that he is leaving the moonlit valley. The same landscape, which is the one the poet wanders through and meditates in, i.e., the simple environment of the lonely man, is simultaneously used as a metaphor symbolizing his mood. The real landscape, the landscape used as a metaphor and the mood of the meditating man are completely fused. The real clue to the poem, however, is given only in the last two stanzas, when the natural scene gives way to the human statement in which a desired, but nonexistent friend—symbolized by the existing moon—"enjoys" what "wanders" (*wandelt*) through the labyrinth of a man's heart. That the poet succeeded in subduing man's inner chaos with the help of the mild moonlit landscape is a great poetic achievement. Glances into this "labyrinth" are clearly present in the poem. We hear not only of man's torment and pain, but also of the river's wintry flood. And yet, the serenity of this night is the dominating feature. The reader feels that, if it were not for the solitude of the man and the gentleness of the moon, the poet would not have exposed the labyrinth. Goethe is not the man to talk lightly of the dark powers whose presence he so often felt. To avoid all outward appearance of chaos, he wrote the poem in tightly controlled trochaic four-line stanzas with regular rhymes and no poetic license whatever. Modern readers are used to finding chaos expressed rather than controlled in a poem, but Goethe controls it by the poetic evocation of the friendly moonscape. Its existence is, nonetheless, the essential counterbalance to the moonlit fields.

IV *The* Roman Elegies

When the poet, almost forty years of age, but more youthful and passionate than ever, returned from his year and a half's stay in Italy, during which he had freed himself from Frau von Stein's emotional bonds, he brought back not only a profound experience of the "South," but also a renewed understanding of the Latin authors he had studied in his youth. Their influence can be seen in Goethe's choice of the elegiac meter for his *Roman Elegies*. It is mainly Propertius from whom the poet took over not only the meter, but also certain poetic passages and images. Basically, he attempted to write "earthy" love poetry devoid of a metaphysical background, a poetry furthermore which would express a simple and happy love affair, unencumbered by grand visions of the universe or deep psychological insights. For this affair the Roman environment would be the fitting background, and the Roman gods would appear as natural as the Roman verse.

Shortly after his return from Italy, Goethe had met the young and pretty Christiane Vulpius, who was a worker in a factory where artificial flowers were made. Goethe took her into his house and many years later married her, after she had borne and raised their children. It shows Goethe's unconventional and liberal mind that he was unfazed by the scandal these actions produced in Weimar. The *Roman Elegies* mirror the happiness and simplicity of this love and are, in their Roman disguise, a lovely compliment to the young woman.

The *Roman Elegies* form a poetic cycle, held together more by the poetic environment of Rome and the Roman gods than by any story line. While the love described here is simple and happy, the poems themselves are complex and rich. The cycle starts with the lonely visitor in Rome; but already the second poem details the first encounter of the lovers and then moves gracefully through the various situations, dwelling on the charm of the young woman and her later pregnancy. Goethe's sense of humor stands him in good stead—and the absence of tragedy is happily felt. A lightness of treatment characterizes the work, a complete mastery of the artistic material, and an artistic distance which enables the author to present his work as though he were playing a game.[15] The absence of anything ponderous, of any "sides" taken, "conflicts" to be resolved, "thoughts" to be expressed, produces the impression of effortless creation which we can expect only of a mature artist.

Rhythmically, these elegies, which have nothing elegiac about them except their meter (hexameters and pentameters), are remarkably successful. The German language tends naturally toward iambic or trochaic meters. But there are, particularly among the adjectives, many two-syllable endings, for which Goethe had a special liking, and that not only when he wrote hexameters. He uses them with great success, e.g., in the hymnic parts of *Faust*. In the Elegies they fall into a natural pattern, such as "Reden feindlicher Menschen," or "dieses liebliche Bild." Many other devices could be listed, all of them causing the hexameter to sound like a native line. Also the caesuras of the pentameters fall into such a natural pattern that only the very attentive reader will be aware of the classic meter. There are few similes because every situation is in itself an image and needs no metaphoric support. Thus, there is a lovely poem (IX) describing how the poet waits at the flaming fireplace for the beloved who, before she leaves him the next morning, rekindles the fire, because, as the last two lines assert, it is her special gift to reawaken joy when it has barely burned out. Goethe's characteristically free treatment of time in this poem—in this case the present and the future are fused—should by now be familiar; and the fire is simultaneously a literal and a metaphoric flame.

V *The Ballads*

In the 1790s Goethe liked to write in hexameters and the elegiac meter,[16] which he abandons, as he had the Pindaric odes, in favor of new endeavors after the turn of the century. However, it would be wrong to claim that hexameters were the dominant feature of his poetic production during that period. Equal in poetic maturity to the *Roman Elegies* are the ballads he wrote, mainly for Schiller's newly founded magazines *Die Horen* and the *Musenalmanach*, where the *Elegies* had also seen their first publication.

The earliest of the ballads were written not only before Goethe knew Schiller, but even before he went to Italy. Two of them, "Der Fischer" (The Fisherman) and "Der Erlkönig" (The Aspen King), although based on well-known folk legends, receive their almost uncanny beauty from Goethe's understanding of the dangerous attraction which certain natural phenomena may have for man. The former concerns the mermaid who lures a fisherman into the depth. The poem works through very interesting contrasts. At the beginning, the fisherman is described as being "cool down to his heart." The nymph then reproaches him for luring the fish out of *their* cool domain into the killing heat of the day and finally draws him into that eternally shaded coolness. It almost seems as if his own cool heart had found its "correspondence" in the watery deep. The third stanza, instead of describing this alluring, cool domain, proceeds, on the contrary, to describe sun, moon and sky as they are reflected in the water. The warmth and beauty of the real celestial world are transformed into the coolness of this pure reflection. At the end of that stanza, the mermaid even tempts the fisherman with the reflection of his own face; he becomes Narcissus although he does not love and contemplate himself, but is drawn by his mirror-image into that world which so fascinates him. The eerie attraction which water has for man could not be more poetically and forcefully expressed. This is the opposite of a simple ballad; it is, rather, the poetic vision of a man who has felt the powerful attraction of the calm surface. How much Goethe's mind was obsessed with water at that particular period of his life is clear from "An den Mond" as well as "Gesang der Geister über den Wassern," the first line of which is like a guideline to "Der Fischer": "Soul of man how you resemble water." It is this resemblance which, in the ballad, surpasses mere similarity and turns into fateful attraction.

The same can be said of the "Erlkönig." The child's experience which in the end kills him is the alluring song of the "Aspen-King" who, from a realistic point of view (which the child's father endeavors to maintain), is nothing but a layer of fog. As in "The Fisher," the awe-inspiring natural phenomenon is turned into an alluring song which those who have ears to hear cannot resist. In both poems, the natural phenomenon is expressed in an entrancing song of love.

In his later ballads, Goethe moves away from nature myths to a more human realm. But in almost all of them, some uncanny nonhuman force plays a dominant part. As we know, ballads, and even art-ballads (in contrast to folk-ballads) appeal to simple minds and to children who have preserved a sense for uncanny happenings that is generally overcome by the more sophisticated. For Goethe this is a welcome feature of ballads, where no one expects rational explanations of irrational events, and where the supernatural occurs next to the purely human.

In many of these ballads, we receive the impression that the poet is the bard who addresses his simple audience. Thus the "Hochzeitslied" (Wedding-Song) begins:

> We like to sing and speak of the count . . .
> Here where you celebrate today his grandson's marriage.

"We" is the bard and "you" refers to the festive assembly which celebrates the wedding of the grandson whose ancestor had the miraculous adventures that are then told in the ballad. And even if there is no such formal address as in this ballad, the tone is almost always that of the bard telling his fairy tale to an audience. Moreover, Goethe, in these poems, delights in the poetic sounds which imitate the action:

> Da pfeift es und geigt es und klinget und klirrt,
> Da ringelt's und schleift es und rauschet und wirrt,

The last characteristic feature of the ballads is their sense of humor. Even in the famous "Der Zauberlehrling" (Sorcerer's

Apprentice), the reader is not worried about the outcome of the
flood which the apprentice has conjured up but cannot control.
The sharply clipped lines of the beginning,

> Hat der alte Hexenmeister
> Sich doch einmal wegbegeben!

are humorous in tone and hardly foreshadow a tragedy.

Or the humor lies in the choice of words:

> Da brach ihr die Tasse so hart an dem Mund,
> Es war ein Greuel zu schauen.
> Verlegenheit! Scham!
> Ums Prachtkleid ist's getan!

In contrast to the fairy-tale ballads discussed so far, there are
a small number of serious ballads which have the tone, the
double meanings, and the metaphysical power of Goethe's greatest poetry. Only two of these were written for the *Musenalmanach* namely "Die Braut von Korinth" (The Bride of Corinth)
and "Der Gott und die Bajadere" (The God and the Courtesan).
One other ballad, "Paria," was written many years later. "The
Bride of Corinth" sings of the young man who spends a bridal
night with the ghost of his fiancée, who had been forced by her
family to become a Christian and forbidden to marry her pagan
lover. But the pagan love prevails and although the bridegroom,
too, must die, the lovers will "hurry toward the ancient gods."
Their sensuous love is stronger than the pale Christian faith,
stronger even than death.

"The God and the Courtesan" tells of the god who, to experience and probe human feelings, has come down to earth to meet
the courtesan whom he makes fall in love with him. For the first
time in her career, she loves, and the god, seeing the ultimate
goodness of her heart, raises her in his arms up to Heaven in a
funeral pyre, similar to the one in the preceding ballad.

The retelling of the story, however, fails to do justice to the
beauty of the verse, the sound of the language and the gripping
quality—we may call it demonic—of the ballads. The reader has
the impression that in these "foreign" stories, the ancient and the
Indian ones, some profound truth can be stated, some archetypal
event which moves the reader because it touches on some uncon-

scious, deep-seated knowledge in him. The vampire and the god who saves the forsaken sinner are such archetypal figures. The ballads—in contrast to the fairy tales, in which human characteristics subdue the inhuman forces—seem to have given the poet a chance to preserve the nonhuman forces intact. Perhaps the freedom from any obligation to accomplish more, either philosophically or morally, than simply telling a story permitted the poet to incorporate the dark forces in the life of man without demanding a purely human solution. Goethe's most important ballads present tragic events without any attempt on the part of the "hero" to fight them. There can be no doubt that this acceptance of powerful forces is as typical of Goethe as are his attempts to overcome and humanize them. What Goethe called the demonic found in the ballads a very appealing, direct and unapologetic expression.

VI *Poems on Scientific Subjects*

If Goethe was capable of writing, at the same time, the entirely imaginary ballads and a much more realistic type of poetry on scientific topics, this is due to his belief that science and poetry are not fundamentally separated activities, but that they work in similar ways toward the same goal of understanding life and nature. Goethe greatly enjoyed putting his scientific insights into poetic form. The best known of these poems is the "Metamorphosis of the Plants."

This poem which stems from the time of the *Roman Elegies*, is written in the same elegiac meter and also addresses the beloved woman of the *Elegies*. The poet points out to her the multitude of flowers in the garden and teaches her to see *in* them the unifying law they all obey, i.e., the law of the metamorphosis of the leaf, which he calls the law of multitude and unity. The flowers, organized according to this law, become, in the poem, simultaneously images and metaphors of the poet's love which, thus, is the crowning point of the created world. The law of multitude and unity appears as the law of both love and nature.

The "Die Metamorphose der Tiere" (Metamorphosis of Animals) is treated similarly. It is a poem written in hexameters and indicates, with the lightest poetic touch, how individual animal organs were developed by nature according to the needs of the animals. But, Goethe insists, the strong development of one organ or limb requires a sacrifice, i.e., the weakening of another. Nature has only a limited "mass" at its disposal and could not possibly create a horn or antlers for the lion whom she has endowed with very strong teeth. At this point, the author has found a parallel between human life and animal life, namely the necessary limitation of their respective materials. He can, therefore, speak freely of the law of unity, which exists in poetry as well as in life because, again, he finds the poet, and man in general, acting according to laws corresponding to those of nature.

> This beautiful concept of power and limit,
> of freedom and law, of flexible order,
> advantage and lack of it should make you happy.
> The sacred muse brings it to you harmoniously,
> teaching with gentle compulsion.
> No higher concept is reached by the ethical thinker,
> by the active man, the rhyming poet.
> A ruler who deserves this name enjoys by it only his crown.

This is a "classical" concept of art, its freedom and limitation, which the author arrives at by observing the animal kingdom.

Another natural phenomenon excited the poet as he read Luke Howard's "Essay on the Modification of Clouds." [17] He wrote a number of poems "In Howard's Honor," which he published together in 1822. What fascinated him in Howard's thinking is the fact that he found names for, and consequently steady characteristics of, the unsteady cloud formations: Stratus, Cumulus, Cirrus, Nimbus. In each of them, the metaphorical power of the cloud is felt together with its actual behavior. What makes the cloud formations so important in Goethe's thinking is precisely their stimulation of the human imagination which, on all levels, accompanies the actions and reactions of the clouds. More even than in the metamorphosis poems we feel that the laws of nature, the moral laws of man and the poetic laws of the poet are basically identical and that nothing lends itself better to poetic usage than the scientist's sober observation of nature. In the case of the poems in honor of Howard, Goethe adds the Indian legend of the god Camarupa (which means "wearer of shapes at will"), who, Goethe explains in a short note to the Howard poems (HA I, 408), can shape and reshape clouds according to his own fancy. The language of these poems is powerful and wholly original, full of neologisms and constantly aware of the double nature of what the poem says. As the last lines of "Nimbus" state: "Speech descends, for it describes, Spirit however soars to where it will remain forever."

VII *Der West-Östliche Divan*

In the last years before Schiller's death and for almost ten years thereafter, Goethe's lyrical production slackened. It is the only prolonged period of his life where the creative flow of his lyrical talent diminished to a trickle. Several reasons for this can be cited. Aside from Schiller's death, which affected Goethe greatly, there were major political upheavals: Napoleon was conquering Germany, and the French Army had entered Weimar and Goethe's house. On another level, we should remember that at that time Goethe worked on *Fiction and Truth* and on the *Elective Affinities* by which his poetic faculties were completely absorbed. None of this is offered by way of an explanation. Creativity in Goethe's life, as probably in that of most authors, is a force that can not be neatly assessed in terms of psychological or intellectual causes.

We know, however, the immediate cause of the resurgence of Goethe's lyrical vein. In 1814 he read the translation by Joseph von Hammer of the Persian poet Hafis (died in 1389) whose collection of poetry, called *Divan*,[18] delighted him, and with whom he felt the close kinship between poet and poet which may span centuries and continents. Goethe started immediately to work on his own collection of poems, called *The West-Eastern Divan*, to which he added a prose part *Noten und Abhandlungen* (Notes and Disquisitions), a group of longer or shorter essays on Oriental life and poetry, as well as literary history and theory. Goethe had studied Persian poetry sufficently to enter into its spirit of gaiety, sensuality and serenity. He also had studied its meters and verse-forms and was able to transpose and adapt them to the German language, in a procedure similar to that used in the *Roman Elegies*. However, what may have fascinated him most is the all-pervasive pantheism, so similar to his own, and the resultant, quite un-Christian, joy of earthly life, in which the divine is happily present.

Goethe's growing collection of poems expanded considerably when, in the autumn of 1814, he met a young woman, Marianne von Willemer, on a trip to Frankfurt, where he visited her again in the following year. She entered into the poetic spirit of the work and contributed some of the poems to the central "Buch Suleika." Goethe, without mentioning her authorship, added her poems (two of them entitled "Suleika") to his collection, rightly expecting that they would be accepted as his own work.

This is not the place to enter into the many elements that make up this cycle composed of cycles.[19] The latter are probably more appropriately called "books"; they are uneven in length as well as quality, and to call them cycles means to give them a degree of perfection to which they do not aspire. They do, however, have a unity of meter as well as theme, and sometimes of sequence, which emphasizes the cyclic character.[20]

Only a few well-known poems will be discussed here. To understand the whole collection and its many implications, the reader would have to study the Persian sources in Hammer's translations. Perhaps more important, he would have to analyze the structure of each cycle and its relation to the whole; he would have to ponder over the recurring themes and images, and to study the various meters and rhyme-schemes. The remarkable balance between the joy of the here-and-now and the far-reaching religious outlook would also need special consideration.

The title itself says more than appears on first sight. While the poet produces indeed a "divan," i.e., a collection of poems, his particular collection spans Oriental and occidental themes, thoughts and feelings. Hidden in it is also the private "east-western" relationship between the beloved and the poet, emerging in an exchange of letters between Frankfurt and Weimar, and expressed in the poems on the east wind and west wind, which carry messages between the separated lovers.[21]

The most important link between East and West, however, is the course of the sun which, symbol of light and wisdom, comes from the Orient to enlighten the occident. The mythologists of Goethe's time had traced all mythologies then known back to India or Persia where God, it was believed, had first revealed himself to man.[22] *Ex oriente lux* had already been Herder's faith, which was then confirmed, time and again, by some of the many Oriental manuscripts deciphered in the first two decades of the nineteenth century. Oriental wisdom flowed from East to West and became for the first time widely known. The East was considered the cradle of mankind, whence God's revealed word had originated.

Conversely, Goethe himself sets out on a West-Eastern journey to drink from the sources of this wisdom. The first poem of the collection, "Hegire," meaning a journey, specifically Mahomet's journey from Mecca to Medina with which the Moslems start the counting of their calendar, and furthermore the pilgrimage of the Moslems to Mecca, set the tone for this spiritual journey, the journey of the entire work and of many of its individual poems. The poet wishes to find his way back to the origin of humanity, where, when mankind was young, it received from God "heavenly knowledge in earthly languages"; and while man's thinking was still narrowly confined, he took the "spoken word" seriously and enjoyed the vastness of his faith. Goethe felt close to the Persian poet because the "spoken word" was, according to eighteenth-century theories on early mankind,[23] always a "poetic word," and Goethe suggests in the last stanza of this poem that the poetic words, east or west, "hover around the gates of paradise in the hope of acquiring everlasting life."

The sun is the major symbol of the collection and is used, like the entire East-West relationship, in various complex symbolic structures. It simultaneously indicates the East-West relationship and the cyclic quality of all life. It also may indicate the lover or the beloved, and appears in conjunction with the moon or the rainbow. Wherever it appears, it does so in a grand manner befitting its unique role as the bearer of light.

The book *Suleika*, in which the sun poems occur, starts with a little motto:

> I thought at night
> That I saw the moon in my sleep.
> But when I awoke
> Unexpectedly the Sun rose.

The first major sun poem of this cycle is a dialogue between Suleika and Hatem. Hatem is Suleika's lover; in its trochaic meter, it alludes to Goethe's own name.[24]

> Die Sonne kommt! Ein Prachterscheinen!
> Der Sichelmond umklammert sie. (p. 67)
> ❁   ❁   ❁

(The Sun appears, a splendid sight.
The sickle-moon embraces it.)

The question at the end of this stanza "Who was able to unite such a pair?" is answered, first, with reference to the Sultan, who made the sun-moon image into a military emblem intended to honor warriors. But in the next stanza it becomes an image of the lovers, the man being the sun encircled by the moonlike arms of the woman.

In almost all the poems (as is particularly noticeable in this one) the symbol stands simultaneously for great and small things, for general and personal ones, or for the universe and the private love. While these poems are undoubtedly love poems, they also have very broad connotations, and while the love remains private and often secret, it is, as a universal phenomenon, connected with God, the world, and history.

The next sun poem, "Hochbild" (High Image), also opens with the word "sun," meaning the sun rising in the east. This time, however, the rainbow replaces the arms of the moon, and a beautiful metaphor is created, with the sun kissing the cloud-daughter's tears until they shine like pearls. The cloud becomes beautiful under his light, but, being sun and cloud, they can never reach each other.

In this poem, as in many others, the worldwide view is kept intact, but the relationship between the cosmos and the personal love is twisted in a way to make it humorous. Many of these poems are written with tongue in cheek, and the symbolic relationship, while taken seriously in the beginning, is smiled at in the end.

As soon as the poet has compared himself to the sun, he finds himself, in the next poem, changed into night and grayness. Even his heart's tears are gray, ("Nachklang" [Echo]). And whereas he still addresses his beloved as his "moon-face," he very unexpectedly experiences the light that radiates from her and in quick succession calls her "my phosphorus, my candle and my sun."

The last of the sun poems, "Wiederfinden" (Reunion), tells the biblical-creation myth in Goethe's own version. It is a poem about separation and pain and, like the previous poems, makes use of its symbolism to encompass God, heaven and earth. As in the other poems, the simultaneity of the symbolic levels gives to his love a peculiarly cosmic significance. As the poet, in

[74]

the new encounter with the beloved, still shudders when he thinks of the past separation, he visualizes the entire creation as a state of separation. When God said "Let there be . . ." the universe with a "pained sound erupted into reality." The elements, originally united at God's heart, fled each other and were driven to immeasurable spaces, as if in wild chaotic dreams. There was no sound, and God was alone; therefore he created the dawn of day, which produces "sounding color" [25] and, with it, love and the yearning of things for each other. Now man and woman, drawn to each other, create their own world, and the new night, the night of love, confirms the new bond which they will not sever by another "Let there be. . . ." In a grand vision, the poet contrasts the night of chaos, which only the sun can overcome, with the starlit night of the lovers, in which both light and darkness are present as symbols of the human lot of joy and pain.

Another important symbol is the ring. It occurs first in a poem from the *Book of the Bard*, which describes such magic items as the talisman, the amulet, the inscription, Abraxas and, finally, the seal-ring. The latter has the "highest meaning in the smallest space," a magic word being forever carved into it. It is, as the talisman stanza tells us, the name of Allah which "inspires man to love and action."

The ring represents the universe and eternity, God's relation to man and man's relation to others. It represents the cycle of life as well as the poetic cycle. The cyclic movement of poetry and, symbolically, of the universe, is movingly expressed in the first stanza of the poem "Unbegrenzt" (Unlimited):

Unbegrenzt
Dass du nicht enden kannst, das macht dich gross,
Und dass du nie beginnst, das ist dein Los.
Dein Lied ist drehend wie das Sterngewölbe,
Anfang und Ende immerfort dasselbe,
Und was die Mitte bringt, ist offenbar
Das, was zu Ende bleibt und anfangs war. (Buch Hafis) [26]

The "you" may refer to Hafis, who is addressed in the third stanza. But in the second stanza it is the mouth of the beloved ever ready to be kissed; and in the stanza just quoted it might be the Creator as well as the poet. As throughout the *West-Eastern Divan*, the cosmic, the personal and the poetic happenings are drawn together in an imagery relating to them all.

The most famous ring poem in the collection is one of the many dialogues between Suleika and Hatem (64). She has dreamed that the ring he gave her slid from her finger and fell into the water. He interprets this by likening the event to the marriage of the Venetian Doge to the sea and sees in it a symbol of her wedding him, the restless wanderer, to her home on the Euphrates. Even in this poem, which does not claim to establish a cosmic relation, the sensation of space and of the east-west relationship within this space surrounds the central event and gives it meaning in a wider context.

It should be clear by now that the entire collection of poems, even those short and more meditative ones I have not discussed, implies some circular arrangement which, although not clearly carried out in every instance, nevertheless underlies the conception of the whole. From the ring image to the path of the sun, and from the celestial bodies to the cosmos which comes from God and returns to Him, the circular movement is always felt. "Beginning and end eternally the same" (Anfang und Ende immerfort dasselbe) is the motto that could be written over the whole cycle, over each individual group and over many of the individual poems. It is the cycle of life which repeats itself eternally, from the growing of a bud to its fading, to the fruit and the regeneration which proceeds from its seed. Or it is the cycle of water that rises from the ocean as a cloud, descends over the land as rain, and returns to the ocean as a river. It is the motion of the stars and the sun around the earth, and the change of day and night due to the rotating earth. In the life of man, this circular movement is expressed less obviously as a circle, but very clearly as a change from one situation to another and back again. What Nietzsche called the Eternal Return, the endless recurrence of each event in life, from which he suffered because it seemed meaningless, is for Goethe a positive factor, an indication of the World Soul which creates, receives the creation back into itself and then recreates it. The individual cycles are symbolic signs of the over-all movement of all life. Not all of them occur in the *Divan*, but enough do to permit this generalization.

A legitimate way of ending the discussion of this group of

[76]

lyrics is a brief analysis of the famous poem "Selige Sehnsucht"
(Holy Yearning) from the *Book Suleika*.

> Selige Sehnsucht
> Sagt es niemand, nur den Weisen,
> Weil die Menge gleich verhöhnet,
> Das Lebend'ge will ich preisen,
> Das nach Flammentod sich sehnet.
>
> In der Liebesnächte Kühlung,
> Die dich zeugte, wo du zeugtest,
> Überfällt dich fremde Fühlung,
> Wenn die stille Kerze leuchtet.
>
> Nicht mehr bleibest du umfangen
> In der Finsternis Beschattung,
> Und dich reisset neu Verlangen
> Auf zu höherer Begattung.
>
> Keine Ferne macht dich schwierig,
> Kommst geflogen und gebannt,
> Und zuletzt, des Lichts begierig,
> Bist du, Schmetterling, verbrannt.
>
> Und so lang du das nicht hast,
> Dieses: Stirb und werde!
> Bist du nur ein trüber Gast
> Auf der dunklen Erde.[27]

Like all the other poems discussed here, this one operates
simultaneously on several levels and symbolically reinforces
Goethe's belief that the particular is mirrored in the universal
and the universal in the particular. As in so many of his poems,
the underlying idea, as expressed in the poetic images, indicates
the unavoidable polarities of life. Thus "the living yearns for
death in the flame" only to be reborn, so that Goethe can turn
the sentence around in the last stanza by saying "die and
become (or live)," thereby completing the circular process.

The fact that man "dies" and is reborn in the act of love is a
commonplace and would be of no interest, if it were not placed
in a large and almost mysterious context. In the first place, time
is eliminated, as it was in the poem "An den Mond" and else-

where. The "love nights in which you procreate and were procreated" subsumes all love nights under one and makes the event of procreation into one ever-renewed cosmic event. Space, too, is eliminated: "No distance is difficult for you." The next contrast we encounter is that between light and darkness. The little candle turns into the Light of God, or the Light of Knowledge, or whatever form the "higher" light may assume. And without this yearning for the light, which the title calls "blessed," man would be in the darkness from which his flight takes off in the third stanza. Without his desire to "die and become," he would only complete a cycle from "der Finsternis Beschattung" to "der trübe Gast auf der dunklen Erde."

A similar contrast is established between heat and coolness. The latter describes the love night which is lit only by the quiet candle. Death in a flame, however, is the result of "höhere Begattung," that procreation and rebirth of the mind and soul which is the true goal of this blessed yearning. And while the image of the butterfly seems to reduce the situation to the material level of the candle, the butterfly is really an image of the soul attracted to the light of God and the true death and rebirth is that which aspires to the "real" light and flame.

The earthly love, although by no means despised, is only a symbol of that higher aspiration whose definition is wisely forgone, and the latter is mirrored and implied in the simple act of love. Thus, the earthly event acquires a depth, a twofold reality, which for Goethe more and more decisively indicates the nature of all earthly events, as being perfectly real and at the same time, perfectly symbolic. It is a very Goethean trait to express these two aspects of earthly life in complete simultaneity. The candle shines on the love night, and without this "real" image there would be no profounder experience. But *in* the "real" image the larger context is contained, and the reader can never limit himself to the one without being profoundly touched by the other.

It is one of the secrets of Goethe's life that he "died and was reborn" so often. The youthfulness of his mind depended on it. His acceptance of this phenomenon, which is simultaneously the phenomenon of all organic life, was one of Goethe's great contributions to what can only indirectly be called the history of ideas. What disturbed many other poets, namely the passing quality of all existence, had an entirely positive aspect for Goethe. "Dying and becoming" was to him the essence of any fruitful human existence. From this point of view, the poem is symbolic of its author's profoundest personal experience. But the impersonal manner in which the experience is expressed in the poem surpasses the autobiographical and raises the poem to the level of universality, even though the "crowd" may never understand the poem or the experience reflected in it.

VIII *Gott und Welt*

In the last edition of his completed works, edited by Goethe himself, the writer grouped his poems under a number of titles, under one of which, "God and World," he gathered the more philosophical poetic works of his late period. The time of their conception spans the last thirty years of his life. They are, in part, poetic expressions of his various studies in natural history while others are more specifically concerned with his Neoplatonic outlook as applied to either natural or human phenomena. What they have in common is a "monumental" style expressing itself in apparent simplicity.

The group starts with one of Goethe's most monumental poems: "Prooemium." Here we no longer find the rich symbolism of his youth, nor is there any definition of space or time: We also encounter fewer sound effects and no reliance on the poetic devise of free rhythms. The poem consists of blank-verse which rhyme in couplets and which might lead us to believe that such a simple scheme is trivial or unoriginal. The opposite, however, is true. The simplicity is that of a poet who, after having used almost all kinds of poetic forms and techniques, has mastered the art of stating the mysteries of life in their directest and simplest way. Although none of the most common artistic devices are exploited, the thought content does not prevail over the poetic expression. To be sure, certain thoughts are expressed, but only poetically so. The simplicity of form and the vastness of content are completely amalgamated and inseparable.

The first line of "Prooemium" affords a perfect example: "In the name of Him who caused Himself to be." Goethe thus introduces the World Spirit, the creative source of all creation. The line is self-contained and constitutes all that Goethe has to say about Him whom he never names. Three times in the first six lines he speaks in the name of this nameless Being who, by His very nature, remains forever unknown.

Creation is this Being's essence and calling, and as He creates Himself (and, we must imply, the world), he also creates faith, trust, love and action in man. And he endows man with the gift of recognizing Him, or rather His image, in everything he hears or sees. It is this image and symbol that attracts man and adorns his life's path. In the contemplation of the symbolic and lovely world, time and space no longer matter, and man's every step achieves that degree of "immeasurableness" which points back to the "eternity" of the poem's beginning.[28] Both His eternity and man's immeasurableness are outside of time. Thus, we might add with a hint at the Faust problem, eternity is contained *in* every fleeting moment.

I have paraphrased the poem in order to show that it is not a truly philosophic one, or, to put it differently, that its philosophic stance would not touch us if it were not presented in its peculiarly grand poetic form. We may even contend that the poem does not contain a philosophic but rather a poetic vision of life. The vision embraces, in fourteen short lines, the creative Spirit, Nature and its particular function in the life of man (to be God's image), and Man, who finds Him in every natural thing and thus overcomes his limitation within time. It is a joyous and religious vision which, without asserting a positive faith, never denies faith. In their monumental simplicity, the words communicate the harmony of the religious vision.

Another of Goethe's pantheistic poems, "Eins und Alles" (One and All) was placed in *God and World* immediately before a poem called "Vermächtnis" (Bequest), which was written many years later but echoes "Eins und Alles" by beginning with the words with which the latter had ended.

The first stanza of "Eins und Alles" (1821) speaks of the limited individual who, in order to find himself in "the limitless," gives himself up and thus overcomes "narrow desires and stern demands." In the second stanza, this individual is penetrated by the World-Soul in order to wrestle with the World-Spirit.[29] Undefined spirits lead him gently to Him who created and creates everything. If these two stanzas are perhaps not as clear as we expect from Goethe's poetry, the next two stanzas make up for it by a particularly rich presentation of Creation.

Nothing created ever remains unchanged—or else it would become "armed with rigidity," which is the very opposite of "eternal, living action." What has not yet been created will be created—thus there will be pure suns and colorful earths. It is the last three lines of the poem that gave Goethe pause and made him write the second poem. "Everything will fall into nothingness if it tries to remain in the state of being." "Being" here means lack of development—the arch-mistake in Goethe's view.

What makes these stanzas so remarkable is their expression of the eternal change of everything that exists. Goethe finds ever new words for this process of re-creation, mostly verbs or nouns derived from verbs—a fitting choice because these verbs express activity: "umschaffen, wirken, ewiges Tun, werden, nicht ruhen, regen, handeln, schaffen, verwandeln." Seen on a large scale, as the "suns" and "earths" clearly indicate, this is indeed the process of all nature, at every moment and for all time. The tension Goethe felt between the achieved form and its ever renewed change has been discussed in the chapter on natural science; it is, in fact, the real problem for a modern man who, as an artist, depends on form, but who, as an observer of nature, feels the impossibility of any natural form being constant.[30]

The rhyme scheme of these stanzas, aabccb, seems to indicate a desire for constancy, since the b-rhymes are masculine and contain such words as "quiet" and "rest." But the other lines have feminine endings and contain the words implying change; and somehow the balance of the poem is in their favor.

As a whole the poem seems to me less perfect than some of the other late poems from Goethe's hands. Goethe does not explain the distinction between World-Soul and World-Spirit and omits any explanation of the good spirits that lead the mind toward Him.[31] Moreover the ascent of the mind toward Him, obviously the theme of the first two stanzas, is not stated clearly in the concluding two, where the mind, having freed itself from the limitations of life, contemplates the created world in its eternal changes. The last two stanzas express a universality which the individual mind of the first two seems barely capable of observing. Yet the poem has its unity in the dissolution of the individual, who overcomes his limits in order to join the grand scheme of the universe.

Compared to this enormous vision, the poem "Heritage" (1829) seems rather pedestrian. It tells man how to live within this grand scheme and comes up with such notions as conscience, the role of reason in sensory perception, and man's modest role in a small group of friends. It was written when Goethe was almost eighty years old, and even the visionary of the universe may have found it comforting to throw a humble glance at a smaller environment. What the poem has taken over from the previous one are the first few lines, and these are written in the grand style of his best metaphysical poems:

Kein Wesen kann zu nichts zerfallen!
Das Ewge regt sich fort in allen,
Am Sein erhalte dich beglükt! [32]

"Being" in this poem, as elsewhere, is the state in which "laws" exist, and no matter how hard Goethe tries to reconcile himself to their existence, "being" for him never has the attraction of "becoming." For Goethe any law—ethical, social and, in some respects, even natural—is associated with constraint, duty, and lack of freedom. He realizes the necessity of such laws, but necessity itself is hateful to his free spirit.

In human life he realizes the duality which is derived from the laws on the one hand and man's desire for freedom on the other. "Urworte, Orphisch" (Primeval Orphic Sayings) expresses this duality most concisely. The five stanzas of this poem have Greek titles, taken from ancient collections of Orphic sayings. The meter is *ottaverime* with the rhyme scheme abababcc. There is no consistency in the use of masculine or feminine rhymes, which elsewhere in Goethe's poems is such a relevant feature.

The tension between "form" and "development" is tersely expressed at the end of stanza 1: "Geprägte Form, die lebend sich entwickelt." (Shaped form that develops like living things.) The "Daemon" of the first stanza indicates, clearly enough, the hereditary "law" which determines man's personality. Goethe uses astrology instead of the more scientific heredity. As it were, the latter was as yet unknown, while in Goethe's work, the former was in suspended animation, i.e., half believed and half used as a nice poetic device.[33]

If the ancient daimon—a concept for which Goethe had a

particular respect—creates and preserves the form and, hence, the law of the personality which, in its over-all aspect, is immutable, the second stanza, "Tyche" (accidental occurence), introduces the changing environment. As always when change and motion are referred to, Goethe uses his favorite word "wandeln" related, as it is, to "verwandeln" (change), but also indicating a gentle motion. By making it a rhyme-word, he can play with it by introducing words which are partly positive (handeln—to act) and partly negative (tandeln—to play around).

The third stanza, "Eros," then introduces the great force of love which, coming down from "ancient chaos," hovers playfully over man on a spring-day. That situation might for a moment be described with Goethe's earlier word "tandeln," but soon the heart feels bound to one love. When this happens, "Ananke" (necessity), becomes stronger than ever, stronger even than the law of the personality "according to which you started out." The fourth stanza consequently plays with the words "wollen" and "sollen" in an almost painful way. To *have* to do what you do not *want* to do is for Goethe always a dire constraint. His freedom, under these conditions, is only an "apparent freedom," and in the fifth stanza he even calls this lack of freedom "widerwärtig" (contrary).

"Elpis" (Hope), is the title of the last stanza, which contains much more than hope. The "being" that moves past the "wall of necessity," weightless and unbridled, and which lifts us above cloud, rain and fog into endless zones should really be called "imagination." Within the frame of the orphic words, the term "imagination" has no place, since it is not an ancient concept. On the contrary, it was formulated and described only by Goethe himself and his contemporaries. While Goethe, the consistent and form-conscious poet, abides by the letter of the ancient terms, his mind soars far beyond these rigid concepts into a realm with which he is only too familiar. Whereas the word "imagination" does not occur, the description of this light spirit is too vivid and its action too far-reaching simply to be considered as hope. Also, Goethe himself would have been very dissatisfied if he had built his life on hope. He required, and always possessed, that freedom of the mind which allowed him to roam in his imagination even when he felt himself bound by social or personal constraints.[34]

What makes this poem great is not the description of man and his ever repeated fate. It is, rather, the fact that Goethe felt certain fundamental facets of human life to be governed by powers he found it easy to describe in terms of "gods" or "spirits." For his poetic mind, the degree of personification of these powers posed no problems. He was careful not to turn them into allegories, but to leave them sufficiently undefined and vague; they are, however, clearly presented as powerful influences. Somehow they remind one of the "middle spirits" of the Renaissance. But they are not placed within any given cosmic order; in fact, they are nothing but certain fundamental forces of human life. Except for Daimon and Ananke, which represent binding laws, they are in motion. In the Ananke stanza, Necessity is not even mentioned, but instead one sees man's will pitched against her. Pain and sorrow are not among the orphic words—only the slight and sweet pain of love is mentioned. To Goethe the worst pain was the "harsh necessity" of stanza four—compared with it all other personal suffering seems to have no cosmic origin or power.

In contrast to the impersonal, universalized presentation of the Life of Man in the "Orphic Sayings," Goethe wrote, under the impact of a last great love, a very personal, individualized poem called "The Trilogy of Passions." In these three poems, the objective view of man's life on earth gives way to a personal memory, a personal love and a separation from the beloved, and, finally, to a personal solution to his sorrow in the experience of music. The monumental style of the *God and World* group of poems is entirely preserved in the "Trilogy" and, as in the *Divan*, the personal experience is elevated to the level of a religious experience. The personal pain, however, still vibrates in each line. Goethe became desperately ill in September, 1823, when he returned from Karlsbad, where he had taken leave of the young Ulrike von Levetzow, the idolized image of the poems. During this illness his friend, the composer Zelter, had to read to him, time and again, these three poems he had written during his trip home from Karlsbad.

The "Trilogy" evokes the memory of two of Goethe's most tragic characters, Werther and Tasso, who had come to grief through their great love. The first poem of the "Trilogy" is addressed to Werther and ends with a line from *Tasso*, which is then used as the motto for the long "Elegy" that forms the core of the *Trilogy*. The poet speaks to Werther, as to an old friend whom he meets again, about the happiness of love and the terror of parting. *Scheiden* (to part) is the key word of the first poem, which rhymes with *leiden*, the suffering which appears in the title of the novel about Werther.[35] In the first stanza, the evening sun is called *Scheidesonne*, and the poet continues:

> *I* was chosen to remain, *you* to depart.
> You preceded me [in death] and did not lose much.

The poet then describes the confused effort with which man, if his fate is to live on, tries to control himself and the world, and he devotes the last stanza to the parting (*Scheiden*) of Werther as well as to his own parting from the beloved, which he calls death; he ends with a slightly modified line from *Tasso*: "May a god give him to *say* what he suffers."

Fortunately for the poet, this *saying* of his pain *is* the poem. The "Elegy," written in even *ottaverime*, combines, as do so many of Goethe's mature poems, the past, the present, and the future. For the latter, i.e., the time after his "Scheiden," his heart has neither the will, nor even a conception of how, to go on living. He feels that the gods who first gave the girl to him are now mercilessly destroying him. Thus the "Elegy" ends, but before this desperate ending the poet creates the image of the Beloved which fills him—at least momentarily—with humility and gratitude. It is in this state of humble acceptance that the poet experiences with a pure heart the reverent piety of which he partook in her presence, the piety dedicated to something Higher, Purer, Unknown, which, in the next moment, he calls the Unnamed Ones. Nowhere has Goethe expressed with greater awe the felt presence of a Being before which man humbles himself. The presence of the beloved melted in his heart what he calls "Selbstsinn," "Eigennutz," "Eigenwille"—the self-assertion of the ego which, if present, makes humility and self-abandonment impossible. In these central stanzas of the "Elegy," the poet compares the peace of love with God's peace on earth, which he experienced in her presence. It is the peace which a profoundly disturbed heart remembers to be the ultimate truth of its love.

The poem is an internal monologue, recapturing the various moods of anticipation, fulfillment, departure and memory. The stanzas are linked by a partial repetition of lines. The even flow of the language is deceptive—it does not prepare the reader for the expression of the almost fatal grief with which the poem ends. As always with Goethe, the form is tight and controls the heart-breaking content.

In the third poem, Goethe finds consolation in the harmony of music. This is the weakest of the three poems and does not carry the conviction of the "Elegy," whose simultaneously grateful and catastrophic tone it does not emulate.

The "Elegy," however, as well as the poem addressed to Werther are perhaps the most deeply felt poems Goethe ever wrote. More so than most of his earlier poetry, they may be called parts of a personal confession. But even in these poems his sense of form prevails; while they are desperate, they achieve a tone of tragic harmony, both in their language and the remembered images of the lost love. Goethe has been criticized for failing to write tragedy.[36] In a mature person with a fundamental faith in the healing power of life, even tragic events, however, can be expressed in harmonious lines and stanzas. If the poetic word is strong enough, as is here the case, the tragedy is not extinguished by the beauty of the poetry. We see an old man, almost dying of grief, who is able to convey this grief with all the power of his poetic mind, which does not desert him even at this critical moment.

IX General Remarks on Goethe's Poetic Techniques

Any generalization on the specific poetic qualities of the lyrical oeuvre of as great a poet as Goethe must fall short of his true achievement. Here will be discussed only a few typical features which are inherent in his peculiar talent and upon which he could draw at almost any time of his life while simultaneously developing them and elaborating on them throughout his life.

The first of these features is an innate sense of what is essentially poetic in language and what is not. Goethe's poetic language is characterized by a sense of sound quite specifically his own and far superior to that of any of his contemporaries, even of Hölderlin, who surpasses Goethe in the domain of imagery. Sound as a conveyor of meaning may be as old as poetic language, but the consciousness of this fact and its aesthetic implications were fully developed only in the nineteenth century. As an aesthetic theory it does not occur in Goethe, but as a conscious poetic practice it is strongly developed. Enough instances have been discussed to indicate the deliberate use of this poetic technique. Goethe's sense of alliteration and assonance needs barely any further discussion.

Actually, Goethe's sense of rhythm is closely related to that of sound. His poems demand oral recitation, and it is not surprising that so many of them have been set to music. What is almost annoying, however, is that his poetry is much more advanced technically, than the music of the composers who loved him most. Schubert, or even Wolff, chose the "even" poems, the rhythm of which can easily be counted and measured. The hymns, hexameters or Persian poems are almost untouched by composers, although in them, Goethe's rhythmical talent shows itself most strikingly. The adaptation of the German language to foreign meters, without doing violence to either the meter or the language, is one of Goethe's most daring achievements, but the admiring composers were too close to the simpler poetry of their own period to understand the rhythmic impact of Goethe's bolder poems.

Goethe's rhythmic sense is particularly striking and effective in the complex rhymes where he shows an unfailing sense not only of masculine or feminine endings—all of them of great importance for the meaning of the poem—but, even more so, for the complexity of German grammatical endings, which he uses to great advantage. While the most remarkable rhymes of this type appear in *Faust*, there are sufficient instances in the poetry to realize what a carefully developed technique this was.

Goethe's imagery is almost exclusively derived from nature and natural phenomena. Being a great observer of nature he created remarkable images based on close observation. Since he saw man himself fundamentally as a natural phenomenon and could not conceive of him in any other terms, his natural imagery is not "imposed" upon man's moral behavior or his violent emotions. On the contrary, all human phenomena have their parallel in natural ones—the correspondence between them being not only poetic, but based on an essential and real relationship. For Goethe's poetry this is an important precondition, although not a philosophic one, since it expresses itself in poetic visions. But it has, of course, a backbone of "Weltanschauung" which Goethe, with his peculiarly thorough and accurate mind, took advantage of by writing simultaneously about man and about nature.

Goethe's early poems are focused on a central symbol, be it a violet ("Das Veilchen"), a Greek god ("Prometheus") or even a natural event ("Mohamet"). With a sure poetic insight, Goethe followed up these symbols and enlarged their possibilities within the poem. In the poems written after his return from Italy, the central symbol ("Römische Elegien") is no longer a single metaphor, but the setting itself becomes symbolic. Rome and Roman life form, as it were, the mythological basis of these poems. The same applies, mutatis mutandis, to the *West-Eastern Divan*.

Goethe's late poems contain no metaphors, but only one central symbol: the creator and the created world. The language becomes simple, translucent, and direct. While the poet does not make his demiurge speak, as Milton does, he makes him act in the grand manner of a creative being. In fact, "creating" becomes the keyword of the entire work. We are faced with a poet who stands in awe of, while simultaneously participating in, the eternal creativity of everything living.

That the process of poetic creativity was also Goethe's earliest concern is evident, not only thematically but, more emphatically, in his poetic practice. It is particularly clear in his many neologisms. The German language permits new word formation of great ingenuity in a manner unknown to English and the Romance languages. Goethe can thus legitimately turn verbs into nouns by adding the neuter article to the infinitive. He likes such neologisms as "das Wandeln" and many others which are quite intelligible to his readers, even if they did not previously exist.

The same type of noun-formation can be produced by adjectives: it must be stated, however, that nouns made by simply putting a neuter article before the adjective have the poetic advantage—sometimes it might well be considered a disadvantage—of being quite indefinite. Since their original function of being modifiers almost forces the reader to look for the finiteness of a following object, these adjectival nouns have a peculiarly indefinite quality; e.g., "Im Grenzenlosen sich zu finden" cannot be translated into English without adding again a noun which Goethe purposely omitted. Goethe, as we have frequently shown, likes precision. When he chooses indefinite nouns, he does so on purpose, as the above line so clearly demonstrates. "The limitless" is precisely what it is, i.e., unlimited. Every noun modified by it, such as time or space, would limit it.

Goethe also created new compound words. From "Wanderers Sturmlied," whose title contains such a new formation, I could quote many such examples. In the first two stanzas alone we find "Regengewölk," "Schlossensturm," "entgegensingen," "Schlammpfad," "Feuerflügel," "Blumenfüsse," "Flutschlamm." [37] Whereas, in his later poems, Goethe was less exuberant in his word-creations, there is hardly a poem altogether devoid of them. Just like the verbal nouns, these are easily grasped compounds, but not every German poet can be said to have delighted as much as Goethe in the sense of creativity which is expressed in these neologisms.

I have discussed a few of the technical devices in order to point out the consistency of Goethe's poetic technique. Others have been discussed in the analyses of individual poems. Language as an instrument is, to be sure, the tool all poets have to work with. Goethe uses "poetic words" i.e., words which immediately address themselves to the poetic imagination of the reader, almost to the exclusion of other poetic means. As a result, his poems are particularly difficult to translate. His ideas, at times, sound trivial if put into a foreign idiom. His imagery may sound repetitious. But none of these possible objections is valid if the poems are read in the original, which is not only original, in the sense that it bears the imprint of Goethe's mind, but also very beautiful. Whatever beauty in poetry may mean, there is no doubt that the reader of Goethe's poetry will feel touched by a quality of language to which the term readily applies. It expresses best the quality of easy flow, musical sound and vibrant life which is characteristic of all of his best poems. We note, furthermore, a complete absence of cheap emotions or trite words; in their place, we encounter a sense of novel expression and rare sensitivity. The repetition of themes, on the other hand, is irrelevant because of the great variety and originality of form so characteristic of this poet.

CHAPTER 4

Plays

I *Introductory Remarks*

WE know from Lessing's famous *Hamburgische Drama-turgie* (1766) how difficult it was for German stage directors to improve the level of performances and to remedy some of the many shortcomings from which the German theater was suffering. Lessing had been employed as a critic of the Hamburg theater in order to reform it, and he had criticized with great sarcasm the choice of plays as well as the performance of actors and the details of staging. One of his main points of attack was the choice of second-rate French plays, which seemed to be the audience's favorites. A few German authors, among whom Lessing himself was foremost, tried to add original German plays to the repertoire, but as late as five years before Goethe wrote his first version of *Götz*, Lessing was still fighting a hard battle against the preference for French plays.

Against these tendencies of the German stage, a new trend made itself felt in literary taste, as well as in the theatre, largely as a result of Rousseau's major publications which date from almost exactly the same period as the *Hamburgische Drama-turgie*. Rousseau's call for a "return to nature" meant among many other things, a complete reversal of existing stage practice, an exclusion of what now came to be considered affectation in favor of a "natural" style of speech and action. The new heroes, too, had to be "natural," unencumbered by the well-known French social conventions.

An additional influence was the French and English tendency to put "simple" people on the stage rather than an aristocracy now considered degenerate. This is not only a question of the "bourgeois theater" demanded by Diderot and others, but, at least in the approximately ten years between *Götz* and Schiller's *Räuber*, of a presentation of the masses as well as of individual characters from the lower classes. Shakespeare's plays, whose first German translation by Wieland had just appeared (1767), served as a model for all these trends and was, as we saw earlier, the great favorite of the young authors who soon found their leader in the young Goethe.

As will be shown later, many of the theatrical problems of this period were presented in Goethe's novel *Wilhelm Meister's Apprenticeship*, written twenty-five years later. Here Goethe describes various theatrical groups and points out some of the many problems encountered by actors in their careers and their personal lives. He also introduced a mature stage director who knows his craft and mocks at the ignorant audience and its uneducated behavior.

Goethe had become well acquainted with plays and actors in his childhood, mainly during the French occupation of Frankfurt in 1759.[1] He had acted himself in amateur productions and had owned a puppet theater. It can be said without exaggeration that the stage always was his main preoccupation.

II   *Götz von Berlichingen mit der eisernen Hand*

Before Goethe became known as a lyricist, his name rose to fame very suddenly with the publication of his *Götz*. The original prose-version, *Die Geschichte Gottfriedens von Berlichingen mit der eisernen Hand* (*The History of Gottfried of Berlichingen with the Iron Hand*) written in 1771, was not published until 1831. Goethe rewrote the play in 1773, calling it *Götz von Berlichingen mit der eisernen Hand*, and published it with the greatest success; it was particularly acclaimed by the young authors known as the writers of *Storm and Stress*, who rightly felt that a great master had forcefully expressed their own rebellious spirit.

Whereas Goethe tried to write a play in the "manner of Shakespeare," he actually created a remarkable folk-play, with a popular hero, a great deal of movement, and a mixture of high- and low-class characters. Moreover the play expressed a theme from the German reformation that strongly appealed to his contemporaries, in that it dealt with the free individual who stands up against a corrupt, hierarchical society. Its language is refreshingly unsentimental, sometimes popular and dialectical, and occasionally even obscene—altogether a play that can be successfully performed even today. In its youthfulness, rebelliousness and strength it is a precursor of Büchner's much more tragic plays, and even the Expressionists could fall back on it.

However, the play does not stand up to close analysis. Its characters do not have sufficient depth, its ideational content is weak, and its action not entirely convincing. Its main weakness lies in the secondary plot, which concerns Götz's sister Marie and her fiancé Weislingen, who wavers between his loyalty to Götz and his family on the one hand and the attractions of the Bishop of Bamberg's court and its main courtesan, Adelheid, on the other. He is a traitor to both sides and largely the cause of Götz's downfall. Unlike Shakespeare's demonic traitors, Weislingen is not driven to treason by witches' songs like Macbeth, or by some innate evil like Iago or the daughters of Lear. He is simply and plainly weak and gullible, easily influenced by his environment, and as such he is an undramatic and, in some respects, even an uninteresting character.

Although Götz's fight for "freedom" is not quite convincing if analyzed too closely, he, in contrast to Weislingen, strikes the audience or reader as a genuine personality, mistaken perhaps, but warm, loyal and honestly convinced of the rightness of his cause. He is an unreflecting character and does not greatly develop during the play, but he has the appealing qualities of the simple-minded, active and upright person whose "drama" could not develop without the treacherous counteraction of Weislingen. He is so essentially German that any comparison with a Shakespearean hero, such as Othello, seems ludicrous. Even his simple-mindedness does not allow for comparison with the Venetian general's monumental ignorance of the human heart. The whole play takes place on the much smaller scale of German sixteenth-century feuds. He is fighting for a freedom understandable only in terms of the sixteenth century, when the Emperor of the Holy Roman Empire had yielded much of his power to the lower aristcracy, against whose sovereignty Götz fights because he feels that his true loyalty is with the Emperor. He wants to be "free from all constraint and all vows," with the exception of those made to the Emperor where, he feels, his submission would be voluntary. Intellectually Götz is not quite capable of understanding the political problem of the freedom which he claims. But his appeal stems less from these problems than from the genuine healthiness and basic goodness of a person who feels more strongly than he comprehends what he is fighting and dying for.

Never again, either in the theater or in his novels, has Goethe created a character of comparable strength. If his characters are unreflecting, like Egmont for example, they are so to the point of blindness; and if they are reflective, as most of them are by nature, they don't have the fundamental moral health which Götz demonstrates so convincingly. Probably the most striking feature of the play is its refreshing and spontaneous language, which omits pronouns and adjective endings, disregards word-order and avoids metaphors. Equally striking is the use of everyday language and simple words, contrasting with the elevated high-flown language of the poems. And yet it is an unmistakably "created" language that is very typical of its author. "Eh man noch ganz droben ist, ist ein Absatz und ein eisern Geländer-lein. . . . (Act I, scene 'Jaxthausen Götzens Burg')."

Goethe continued to write plays in prose for another fifteen years before he turned to blank verse and a more elevated style. But none of these plays (*Clavigo, Stella,* etc.) display the spontaneity of language found in *Götz.* In fact, Goethe's early prose style becomes affected and full of his own clichés. From the point of view of his poetic development, it was time for him to find a new idiom suited to his mature years.

In his first years in Weimar, Goethe started a number of plays without finishing a single one. He wrote them first in prose, took them along to Italy, and reworked some of them in blank verse. Whereas he pretended that he had no time to finish them while serving the Duke, his true reason seems to have been precisely the problem of style. His development took him away from his earlier popular style. Many critics have deplored this fact, without realizing that each phase in the career of an author has its own stylistic demands which dictate to him any needed changes. Personally we may prefer one stylistic period to another, but we should give credit to the author's honesty when he feels that his present style no longer meets his aesthetic demands.

III Egmont

The only one of his half-written plays which Goethe finished in prose after his journey to Italy is *Egmont* (1787). In this particular instance, the reason for the choice of prose is obvious: *Egmont* is, like *Götz*, a drama in which the people play a major role—in fact a much larger role than in *Götz*. Egmont is, truly and importantly, the people's hero. It is his uncritical reliance on this fact that blinds him to the court intrigues to which he succumbs; in other words, it is his blind reliance on being the people's choice that causes his downfall.

The popular scenes are still written in the popular style characteristic of Götz's language. But Egmont's own speech, as well as that of all the characters connected with the Court of the Princess-Regent, is elevated, normalized, less colorful and more refined.

If Götz can be said to have a tragc flaw, it would be his infinite and loyal trust in his friends. Much more so than in *Götz*, this almost moving confidence becomes, in *Egmont*, a flaw of character; it implies a neglect of the realities of political life, a negligence with regard to warning signals, such as the words of both friend (Wilhelm von Oranien) and foe (Alba). It is less a confidence in his friends, than an arrogant trust in his own fate, a hubris which causes Egmont's death. Egmont does not see the dangers because he feels himself immune to them. Götz is a humbler character, and the audience does not expect him to see through political intrigues, but Egmont is an elevated figure, who is well acquainted with the whims of royalty. His blindness is truly a flaw in his character, and his downfall is, therefore, the expected outcome. From this point of view, he is the more consciously formed tragic character.

But Goethe was very anxious to show Egmont in a special light and therefore did not make full use of the tragic possibilities which such a character offered. Goethe was interested in showing him as the darling of fate and of his fellowmen, in making him a radiant and irresistible character rather than pouring the gloom of tragedy over him. As a result, the play is considerably less dramatic than it could have been. Even in the last scene, Ferdinand, the son of his enemy Alba, stands admiringly before Egmont, just as, earlier, the population of Ghent and, above all, Klärchen, his beloved, had stood before him. Through all of this adulation, which is, in its own way as blind as Egmont himself, he is able to uphold his faith in being fate's favored child. After a scene in prison, in which he becomes gloomy and depressed, Ferdinand's unexpected love lifts him again up to that spirit of profound serenity which makes him beloved by everyone he meets. The only person who is unaffected by this charm, but all the more anxious to help him out of his untenable position, is Wilhelm von Oranien, whose words of warning Egmont promptly rejects. He is used to friendship, love and adoration and cannot understand a true friend's critical attitude.

It is easy to criticize the play on two levels. First of all, its hero is too much dependent on worship and therefore not quite worthy of the greatness Goethe confers on him. The other criticism refers to the plot, which could have been much more dramatic if Egmont's radiance had not been quite so much emphasized.

But while this criticism is certainly valid, and while it must be admitted that *Egmont* is not an altogether successful play, there is something rather moving in the way Goethe portrays his character. In all the scenes in which Egmont stands in the center of interest, whether present or absent, the audience is imperceptibly drawn to him by those who admire him lovingly and uncritically. There is something very attractive in a radiant personality, and Goethe made Egmont attractive indeed. We do not criticize his recklessness, but admire his supreme confidence. Even in the scene with Oranien, who advises him to leave the city when Alba arrives, we feel more sympathy with the man who refuses to let caution guide him than with the true friend who accepts caution as a fact of political life. The joy of life, the courage to face dangers, are refreshing and unconventional features; but while Egmont cannot weigh political actions, he also does not weigh the political value which his own preservation may have for the burghers of Ghent. He is best characterized by his famous lines about the Sun horses of time: "Whipped by invisible spirits, the Sun horses of time elope with the light carriage of our fate. And we can do nothing but, courageously and calmly, hold the reins and steer the wheels, left or right, past a rock or a fall. Where do we go, who knows? We barely remember whence we came." (Act II, Scene II)

IV   *The Classical Plays*

Had Goethe continued to write political tragedies without presenting the real conflicts that political life produces, namely the corruptibility of the great in whose downfall Schiller was so profoundly interested, he would have continued on a wrong path. But his good sense led him to write about conflicts of a more personal nature, and in these human problems Goethe found adequate dramatic tension. He never became a first-rate playwright, and his international fame is not due to his plays (with the exception of *Faust*), but he found a more genuinely dramatic vehicle of expression. In the plays of his maturity he loses an important aspect of *Götz* and *Egmont*, namely the broad and lively folk-scenes, the sense of the leader in the midst of his people. What he gains, on the other hand, is a greater depth of character and a better understanding of the relationship of character and plot to the tragic outcome. This does not mean that Goethe's later plays are more "effective" as stage-plays. On the contrary, the liveliness of the earlier folk-scenes is felt by the audience to be a real asset because they enliven the spectacle. The later plays have more of an "inner" action and are not "good shows." They do, however, have the more stringent relationship between plot and character that was just mentioned, something almost "accidental" in *Götz* and *Egmont*.

V Iphigenie auf Tauris

Iphigenie is not a tragedy, but is rather a play in which conflicts are resolved. This does not make it less moving; on the contrary, conflict and pain loom large throughout the work, and their resolution is not joyful. Separation and self-sacrifice make the action painful, and while, ultimately the reader is grateful that the conflicts are overcome rather than carried out to the bitter end, he is also very much aware of the new pain created by the solution and the past pain which has caused the conflicts. It is a subdued play which, till the very end, creates in the audiences a growing awareness of pain and strife rather than exuberance or happiness. In its final version, written in unusually beautiful blank verse, it is a very well balanced and mature work, meant to be understood by a mature audience. Its heroine does not have the naive appeal of a Götz or the lighthearted one of an Egmont. She appeals to human beings who have suffered, survived and learned by their suffering. This produces a kind of catharsis, both in the characters and the audience, which, while being brought about by tragic suffering, does not entail the penalty meted out by tragedy. It ends in a quiet and resigned harmony, in which conflict and pain may be revived by the slightest provocation. The solution is precarious and so is the balance maintained in the work.

Each character, except that of Orestes' unthinking friend Pylades, bears his own conflict, and each conflict is resolved in an individual way, although all solutions are touched off by Iphigenie. The first character with a conflict all his own is Thoas, the barbarian king. He was barbaric but whole before Iphigenie was brought to his shores by the goddess Diana; and it was Iphigenie who engendered in him the desire to be humane, instead of mindlessly killing all foreigners who reached the shores of Taurus. From him the greatest self-sacrifice and resignation is demanded in the end: to give up Iphigenie, whom he wants to marry, and yet to retain the lesson of humanity she has brought to his shores. His pain is very tangible in the end when he turns away from her with the shortest "good-bye." Fate has taught him a lesson but deprived him of the happiness he hoped to achieve in return. It would almost be more plausible to see him fall back into his barbaric habits than to accept a humanitarianism for which there are no rewards except the good deed itself. Thoas becomes nobler in the end, but less strictly human. In his character, psychology is suppressed for the sake of a higher morality, and a twentieth-century audience might be suspicious of the duration of this hard won humanity.

The second character torn by conflict is Orestes, who is insane, i.e., persecuted by the Furies for having killed his mother. After a last, terrible attack of insanity, he is cured in the arms of his newly found sister. It is entirely plausible that the fact of finding her has a profound influence on him, but it is considerably less plausible that his conscience, which has haunted him so violently, should suddenly have been assuaged. If Goethe had in mind his own experience and the idea that time—as it does in *Faust*— heals even a bad conscience, he does not say so. In the play, the mere presence of Iphigenie has a healing effect on her brother. Again, while we understand his sufferings, we simply record his cure brought about by the presence of his almost holy sister.

Iphigenie, who has become what she is by the pain she experienced when many years ago she was separated from her family and country, also has to put her hard won humanity to a severe test. Her conflict forces upon her a choice between saving her brother by means of a lie, or being truthful to Thoas and perhaps sacrificing her brother. But whereas this is a very real conflict, it seems clear from the beginning that she will not have to embrace either of these terrifying alternatives. A woman who has made herself into a kind and generous person at the expense of personal happiness is not likely to fall into the traps set by a blind fate. Since she has demanded much of herself, she can expect self-control and sacrifice from others. Yet, our modern mind, much more open to human frailty and less willing to trust strength of character, is struck by the power of her humanitarian behavior. Like all the other characters, Iphigenie obeys psychological necessity or motivation less than ethical demands. Tragedy would result only from a rejection of these demands, not from their fulfillment. But tragedy would have ended in some glorious defeat rather than in a painful victory.

We have to look at the untragic solution in terms of the eighteenth century. What the German thinkers had learned from the enlightened spirits of their time was a belief in the perfectibility of man. If man is not naturally good, he can learn to be so if he goes through suffering and matures through it. This is the "moral lesson" which we are expected to learn from Lessing's *Nathan der Weise* as well as from *Iphigenie*.[2] The characters in these plays are psychologically motivated only as long as they suffer. The demand of humanity placed upon them by the faith in man's perfectibility surpasses the realm of mere psychological truth in favor of a moral obligation[3] which, if obeyed, forces them into the nobler attitude of forgiveness and kindness.

However, it would be wrong to assume that these plays, most of all *Iphigenie*, were written simply to "educate" an audience. Their "moral" lesson is very subtle and what really happens in the play is of immediate and urgent concern to the characters themselves. Their profoundest problem—and this is true for Thoas as well as for Iphigenie and her brother——is that all of them live in complete isolation and are fully aware of it. Iphigenie and Thoas complain loudly about their loneliness, and from the effect Iphigenie has on her brother it is equally clear that his companion Pylades was not the person to relieve Orestes' isolation. Thoas has lost his son, Orestes and Iphigenie their country. Also, at the beginning of the play they have little or no knowl-

edge of each other. When Iphigenie in the first act reveals to
Thoas her family background, concealed from him through many
years of silence, she starts with this confession a chain of events
the outcome of which she cannot foresee. She does not proceed
out of a complete trust in the king, but rather in the hope that by
hearing her terrible truth he might refrain from marrying her.
Her motivation, at this point, is not simply the desire to be
truthful.

The next step—and this is not a conscious revelation—is
Pylades' account of Agamemnon's death. Of course, this is essential information for Iphigenie, but it is of a different order from
the long kept secret she has just revealed to Thoas. Only in Act
III, when she asks the "stranger," Orestes, about her brother,
the latter confesses to her, although in the third person, the mur-
der of Clytemnestra. It is a first step toward bringing those two
apparent strangers closer to each other; and shortly afterward,
Orestes rejects Pylades' clever lie about him and reveals his
identity to Iphigenie. Iphigenie is now in full possession of her
brother's terrible truth, as Thoas is fully informed about the terrible past of her family. Truth is beginning to prevail. In the
same scene, as Orestes falls back into insanity, she betrays the
secret of her identity to him and, after a last desperate struggle,
he reawakens cured.

From the preceding, it should be evident that only truth, and
the whole truth, can save these tortured hearts from their solitude. Iphigenie realizes this when she says to herself in Act IV,
scene 3:

> The firm ground of your solitude you must
> Abandon now! And once again embarked,
> The waves will take you in their rocking, sad
> And fearful you will not know the world and self.

By giving up her solitude, she also must relinquish her purity,
so she fears, so that for a short time the confessions of truth
seem to have been in vain. They have not helped her because the
most important confession has still to be made. In scene 3 of the
last act, she overcomes these fears and tells the king about
Pylades' and Orestes' plot of leaving secretly with her, taking
along the statue of the goddess Diana. Only when everything
and everybody is revealed in complete truthfulness can a solu-

tion be found and human beings be united. Even Thoas bows to the purification which the dreadful house of Tantalus will finally undergo through the return of his last descendents to Greece.

Whereas in most ancient tragedies the revelation of truth produces tragedy, in Goethe's play the stark terror of Tantalus' family is slowly overcome by a complete revelation of all past horrors; and the drama consists not of terrible acts, but of the dramatic revelation of past deeds, which, hopefully, will lead to peace and purification. The play, however harmonious its ending, is filled with terror, pain and loneliness. Past tragedy is still felt trembling, much more so than in the ancient plays, such as Aeschylus' *Eumenides*, where it is totally relegated to the past. At the end of Goethe's play, our heart is heavier than when the gods in Aeschylus resolve the same problem of the Tantalus family. In Goethe's play, the gods exist only in the human mind, and the solutions have to be found exclusively by the very vulnerable human heart.

From the point of view of language, *Iphigenie* is a lyrical play. For the first time, the German language is completely adapted to a smoothly flowing, poetic-sounding blank verse. Inserted among these even lines are a number of song-like rhythms, such as Act I, scene 4, whose lines have only four accented syllables, and which are written in dactyls; or Orestes' talk to the Furies, with a related, partly dactylic line. Act IV starts with free rhythms, and ends with Iphigenie's famous song to the *parcae*, which, while having a "regular" rhythm, is divided into stanzas with uneven lines. It must be counted among Goethe's greatest lyrical hymns.

The similes are, as always, taken from nature and, as always, they are based on original observation rather than on poetic tradition.

> So haben Tantals Enkel Fluch auf Fluch
> Mit vollen wilden Händen ausgesät!
> Und gleich dem Unkraut, wüste Häupter schüttelnd
> Und tausendfältgen Samen um sich streuend,
> Den Kindeskindern nahverwandte Mörder
> Zur ewgen Wechselwut erzeugt! [4]

Particularly striking is the drawn-out image which Orestes uses after he feels cured.

Lass mich zum erstenmal mit freiem Herzen
In deinen Armen reine Freude haben!
Ihr Götter, die mit flammender Gewalt
Ihr schwere Wolken aufzuzehren wandelt
Und gnädig-ernst den lang erflehten Regen
Mit Donnerstimmen und mit Windesbrausen
In wilden Strömen auf die Erde schüttet,
Doch bald der Menschen grausendes Erwarten
In Segen auflöst und das bange Staunen
In Freudeblick und lauten Dank verwandelt,
Wenn in den Tropfen frischerquickter Blätter
Die neue Sonne tausendfach sich spiegelt,
Und Iris freundlich bunt mit leichter Hand
Den grauen Flor der letzten Wolken trennt:
O lasst mich auch in meiner Schwester Armen,
An meines Freundes Brust, was ihr mir gönnt,
Mit vollem Dank geniessen und behalten.
Es löset sich der Fluch, mir sagts das Herz.
Die Eumeniden ziehn, ich höre sie,
Zum Tartarus und schlagen hinter sich
Die ehrnen Tore fernabdonnernd zu.
Die Erde dampft erquickenden Geruch
Und ladet mich auf ihren Flächen ein,
Nach Lebensfreud und grosser Tat zu jagen.[5]

It is typical of Goethe that he uses the entire cycle, from the thunderstorm to the fertility of the fields after the storm, to describe Orestes' sickness, the gods' anger and his recovery. Enjambement, or the lack of it, is carefully chosen to accentuate the meaning of the sentences, and so are the caesuras. The language is as refined and harmonious as Racine's French is in his best plays. Although the German blank verse has fewer rules than Racine's Alexandrines, Goethe does not permit himself liberties other than the insertion of the song-like passages discussed above, which are all related to the gods. Otherwise he strictly adheres to blank verse, which only Lessing in his *Nathan der Weise* had used before him, and which Goethe turned into a beautifully sounding, rich and smooth dramatic line.

VI   Torquato Tasso

Goethe's greatest tragedy—and here we are dealing with a truly tragic work—was begun a few years after the first draft of

Iphigenie, and finished only after the poet's return from Italy. If, in *Iphigenie*, the close relationship between brother and sister is a reminder of Goethe's own relation to his sister and if Iphigenie's humanitarian outlook was certainly timely, *Tasso* reflects some of the irritations which necessarily arose between the poet and the Weimar Court. But the play does not need explanatory support from anything outside itself. This is equally true for Goethe's knowledge of Torquato Tasso's life.[6]

The play has one feature in common with *Iphigenie*, and exaggerates it even further: Goethe often (perhaps too often) generalizes in a line or two on topical events. Those are the lines which the German public picked out of his works and quoted as Goethe's "wisdom." In a way, the works of this period invited such behavior. Such lines as "man is not born to be free" (II.1) occur frequently. It is the generalization derived from Tasso's particular situation at that moment into a general insight into the situation of mankind that makes such lines suspect to us. What Goethe tried to do in his so-called classical period, namely to raise the particular case to a level where it is universally valid, is something we carefully try to refrain from doing. Statements on "der Mensch" in general do no longer have the appeal to us which they had in the eighteenth century when general ground rules on human behavior were urgently needed to replace the religious view of man which was being lost. Goethe himself seems to have been wary of becoming too fond of an aberrant individual. For him there existed a grave necessity of seeing such a person or situation or event in terms of what might be true for all humanity. His language reflects this concern.

Thus it is all the more astounding to see that in *Tasso* he created a uniquely individual character and situation. As far as I know, this is, the first work in European literature which presents an artist as a "tragic hero." It precedes the Romantic concern with the artist figure, and anticipates that of the later nineteenth century. More and more, poets became interested in, and absorbed by, the creative process and the strange effect it has on the artist himself. In this sense, *Tasso* is the first profoundly self-observing work of modern literature, and in its awareness of the dangers inherent in the artistic life it is a very modern work.

Tasso moves, during one crowded day, from the supreme bliss of being crowned by Leonora d'Este, his beloved princess, for having completed his great work *Gerusalemme liberata* to the loss of her and the utter ruin of his personality. There is no catharsis in this play. It relentlessly puts before our eyes the disintegration of personality at the moment of glory—which, by necessity, is also the moment of greatest vulnerability in a man whose precarious psychological balance is held together only as long as he writes. In this respect, we get a frightening and an utterly unglorifying view of the artistic mind. Tasso's past human weaknesses are, one by one, revealed to us and confirm our judgment of his present unbalanced behavior.

To enhance the tragic atmosphere, Goethe has placed in Tasso's mouth two images, both of them referring to the artist and both relating him to death. The first (I, 3) is, like so many others in the play, part of a poetic dream, something the poet's imagination creates in the presence of his friends, of whom he becomes completely oblivious. Crowned as he is, he sees himself—in his imagination—in the pure mirror of a spring and asks himself: "Who is the deceased man?" And he wishes to be joined at that spring by all the great poets of the past, as Alexander the Great tried to join Achilles and Homer in Elysium. The princess' friend Leonore has to awaken him from his utter oblivion. This is not only the Narcissus image, which becomes the central symbol for the poet throughout the nineteenth century, it is also the dream-wish of the young poet to join the greatest poets of all times—and those encounters traditionally take place in an afterlife.

The second image (V, 3) is that of the silkworm which keeps spinning his silk cocoon until he has entombed himself. Like the worm, the poet cannot help creating even if it costs him his life. And he is not as certain as the worm that in a new, sunny vale he will reappear as a butterfly.

The two images strikingly express a death-wish and it is significant that the former occurs at the moment of the poet's initial happiness. Moreover, it is placed at the last moment of this bliss because only seconds later his antagonist Antonio, the reserved and unartistic courtier, appears on the stage.

The dream-like state of creation—an idea so dear to the romantics—is here presented for the first time. Twice more, the poet loses himself, much more than the present situation requires, in a poetic reverie. The first is an extensive description of the golden

age (II, 1), very much in the style which the historical Tasso
might have used. The second occurs (V, 4) shortly after the
silkworm image. It is a remarkably psychological presentation
which starts from Tasso's actual plan to visit his sister and turns
into a complete and very concrete description of the future visit
as if it were a thing experienced in the past.

> Wo wohnt Cornelia? Zeigt mir es an!
> Cornelia Sersale? Freundlich deutet
> Mir eine Spinnerin die Strasse, sie
> Bezeichnet mir das Haus. So steig ich weiter.
> Die Kinder laufen nebenher und schauen
> Das wilde Haar, den düstern Fremdling an.
> So komm ich an die Schwelle. Offen steht
> Die Türe schon, so tret ich in das Haus—[7]

The princess to whom these words are addressed sees "the
danger in which you find yourself," but she does not interpret
it quite correctly. She sees in it only a self-centered attitude and
ignores the proximity of insanity which is felt with increasing
intensity in this last act.

Fortunately for our image of Tasso, the first act presents him
as a lovable, although erratic, character. We receive the last
glimpse of a noble, generous, and humble man who remits his
finished work only hesitantly to the Duke of Ferrara. That his
sensitivity, to which he owes his talent, is, simultaneously, the
cause of his downfall is more surmised than clearly seen at the
beginning. However, his flaws as a man are pointed out very
early in the play. Already in the second scene of Act I, the Duke,
Alfonso, starts his remarks about Tasso with a criticism: "It is
an old fault that he seeks loneliness more than society." This is
one of the central problems in the drama. A few lines later,
Alfonso bemoans Tasso's hesitation to finish his work and continues by saying that the poet must learn to go beyond the narrow
circle of the Ferrara court to hear "praise and blame." While this
criticism of Tasso characterizes Alfonso and Antonio as essentially
"social" men, it remains nevertheless true that the poet, who had
a difficult childhood, shies away from public life and knows
human beings only imperfectly. This is not truly a character flaw,
but it indicates the spot where Tasso will be vulnerable. In this
scene, the Duke first mentions Tasso's suspicious nature.

> Begegnet ja,
> Dass sich ein Brief verirrt, dass ein Bedienter
> Aus seinem Dienst in einen andern geht,
> Dass ein Papier aus seinen Händen kommt,
> Gleich sieht er Absicht, sieht Verräterei
> Und Tücke, die sein Schicksal untergräbt.[8]

At the beginning of Act II, after the first unpleasant encounter with Antonio, Tasso feels that he is more than usually divided within himself and that the resulting confusion has the harsh quality of an inner conflict. The man and the poet in him are not at peace with each other. In Act III, Scene 4 Leonore describes to Antonio Tasso's impossibility of taking care of his daily needs, of holding on to his possessions. And although she finds his helpless absent-mindedness lovable, Antonio regards it as a flaw.

The last of his minor, but typical flaws is brought up by Antonio (V, i) in a particularly nasty, but presumably accurate, description of Tasso's lack of moderation in matters of food and drink and his refusal to accept a doctor's advice. Tasso is thus described as a spoiled child without self-discipline.

To these more external and superficial bad habits the more severe psychological problems are added. In Tasso's permanent state of creative frenzy his observations of the behavior of those around him are characterized by vast exaggerations. Although these observations start from real facts, they get all too quickly out of hand. The first such violently exaggerated speech he delivers (II, 2) after he has found out that the princess loves him:

> O if the noblest of all feats would here
> Present itself before me visibly
> Ringed round with grisly peril! I would throw
> Myself upon it, gladly risk the life
> That I now have from her hands—I would challenge
> The finest human beings as my friends [9]
> To come with noble forces and perform
> Impossibilities upon her beck
> And call.   (Passage, p. 37)

His dangerous lack of stability is immediately felt, and the audience fears for a man with his lack of a firm grip on reality.

As the play continues, these wild exaggerations characterize each of his reactions to his environment, and they increase with his growing confusion. At the end of the fourth act, he speaks a long soliloquy in which he analyzes—so he thinks—each of the characters around him and the effects they have had on his life. The speech ends with the wild accusation that the princess, too, has betrayed him. The contrast of these two soliloquies concerning the princess is a study in the behavior of an unstable mind.

Closely linked to these fanciful exaggerations is Tasso's growing suspicion of everyone, which, in turn, is an expression of his paranoiac personality. That this growing imbalance is well prepared by Goethe was already seen in the first lighthearted examples mentioned by the Duke in the first act. Goethe, otherwise not overly prone to dwell on psychological problems, has presented in *Tasso* a masterly "case." It starts with suspicions against the servants and ends with the conviction that he is persecuted by his closest friends, including his adored princess. The imbalance of the personality which accompanies such feelings shows itself most strikingly in Act V when Tasso wildly embraces the princess in a kind of rebound from his suspicions.

It must be stated now that Goethe was, of course, far from having any psychiatric knowledge of these emotional conditions. He relied exclusively on his intuitive observation. That this observation, as well as his intuition, came so close to what modern psychiatry knows about such cases must be attributed to his own experience and the dangers he felt himself to be exposed to.

The work would not be a drama however, if it were simply a case history rather than a web of action, reaction, and counteraction. The plot is advanced through the other characters in the play who surround Tasso and interact with him and with each other. The complexity of the plot is considerable, and every character is given his own marked personality.

The duke, the one single person who can do most to help or harm Tasso, is basically a kind, perhaps even generous person, but he is not motivated by any special liking for either the man or the poet. He overlooks Tasso's unconventional behavior largely because he needs a great court poet for his own glory. His true esteem goes to a man like Antonio who is less effeminate and considerably more useful. But he tolerates Tasso's presence and would not even punish him after Tasso draws his sword against Antonio, had Antonio not suggested it to Alfonso. He is indulgent even then by confining Tasso to his own room, releasing him soon afterward. A kind indifference characterizes his behavior toward Tasso, and a disciplined, even temper makes him more princely than anyone else at the court.

His sister, equally aristocratic in her outward behavior, is a much more interesting character. Sickly as a child, she grew up in solitude and became educated and open to poetic expression. In the entire play she is the only one who understands Tasso's behavior and, more important, the dangers pressing ever closer in on him. And yet, although far from wanting to hurt him, her mere existence endangers him. Being herself a sensitive person, she prefers to listen to others in silence or to respond with only a few words. In his presence, however, she opens up, and it is she, not Tasso, who first touches on the delicate subject of their relationship. In Act II, Scene 1 she tells him that he was the first person she met after her long sickness: "Then I was hoping much for you and me; and hope has, so far, not deceived us." At the end of this scene, she almost confesses her love to Leonore Sanvitale, giving herself away to a very watchful, clever woman.

It is always said that the princess is a pale, unemotional character. The play, however, does not bear out this criticism. Her sense of propriety is that of a truly aristocratic woman who hates vulgarity. Tasso is the first to understand this, and he bends to it as to a law of society he would not normally rebel against. He tries to embrace her only at the end of the play at a moment of his complete derangement. On the other hand, she is, aside from Tasso, the only character with strong personal feelings; three times during the play, her heart speaks clearly and intelligibly. It is her openness rather than her reserve which creates a turmoil in Tasso's heart. Had she been less frank, he would not have undergone the agonies of happiness and despair which upset his balance. Part of Tasso's tragedy is precisely the confessed love of the princess against which he has no inner defense.

Leonore Sanvitale is easily understood. She is envious of the court of Ferrara for "owning" Tasso and plays her own little intrigue to lure him away. She is also a trifle jealous of the princess, to whom, as she well knows, the love poems found in the garden of Belriguardo are addressed, and she tries to convince her, quite unsuccessfully, that the poet's love is not of this earth.

She is clever, coquettish and quite untragic. The princess as well as the duke treat her nicely with gentle irony.

Antonio is the real antagonist in the play and he is well chosen. He has a rough exterior, but he is useful and a good politician. As Tasso so rightly observes, the Graces were absent at his cradle when the other gods brought him gifts. (II, 1) His behavior with regard to Tasso shows that he, too, is vulnerable: he is envious of the laurel wreath with which the princess has crowned Tasso. The young poet visibly grates on his nerves. There is a certain rudeness in all his words to and about Tasso, and he expresses a great deal of outspoken criticism even in the last scene of the play when he is touched by the poet's misery. Nowhere does he pretend to understand the emotional troubles to which the poet's mind succumbs. He sees only the immature and undisciplined behavior of a young man who does not deserve the duke's favor. To say that Antonio is either right or wrong in his behavior and his judgment of Tasso is missing the point of the play. Antonio is, like Tasso, in a state of constant reaction, and his reactions become less violent only late in the fifth act when his opponent is clearly defeated. While he is, at times, mean, even meanness is not a prevailing character trait of his. It, too, is a reaction rather than an action.

We are now faced with a discussion of the last scene of the play, which finds Tasso in Antonio's care, after the rest of the friends, contrary to their original plans, return to the city, and Antonio, contrary to his plans, remains in Belriguardo. To see in Tasso's famous last speech some form of reconciliation between the two antagonists seems to me to contradict the entire play. On the contrary, the last speech, with its beautiful comparison between the poet and the waves, and Antonio and the rock against which they break, only confirms what the play has been working up to throughout: "Mighty nature, which founded this rock, has also given to the wave its mobility." Throughout the play, the poetic talent has been considered as a gift of nature. This idea is extended here: not only the aesthetic gift of the poet is nature's gift, but also the moral gift of self-discipline of which Antonio is so proud—and wrongly proud because his self-discipline was not strong enough to overcome his envy of the poet's "easy" victories. But the image does not end here: after the comparison of the wave in which sun and stars are reflected, it suddenly shifts, and the poet is unexpectedly compared with the shipwrecked pilot who holds on to the rock. Whereas, up to this moment, the comparison was not made in the first person, Goethe suddenly shifts: "bursting, the bottom (of the boat) tears open under *my* feet." It is the man, not the poet, who is compared to the pilot, and it is the man, not the poet, who holds on to Antonio. The image seems to indicate what the whole play has been saying, namely that this particular poet, Tasso, has a truly divided personality, and that, after the completion of his work, the poet disappears and the man breaks down. If there is any reconciliation, it is not one of hope, but of utter despair.

The problem mentioned above and often considered central to the play, namely the incompatibility of the poet and the society surrounding him, will have to be restated after what has been said. It is certainly not society, despite its varying and, sometimes superficial, code of behavior, which brings about Tasso's ruin. At most, it precipitates it. With great psychological insight, Goethe has placed the tragedy not between the poet and society, but in the conflict residing in the poet's own heart. The lively and sensitive imagination which produces the work of art is simultaneously the cause of a false, or at least exaggerated, evaluation of reality on the part of the poet and thereby leads to his psychological ruin. His poetic interpretations, as well as his all too human misinterpretations of reality, are so closely related in the work that society cannot play any role except that of a catalyst. This it does consistently. But any generalizations about the role of the artist in a society that does not understand him should be avoided, if the play is to be considered as a unique manifestation of Goethe's own profound experience.

A word must be added on the language. Very consistently Tasso speaks in a lively metaphorical language. In contrast to that of most of the other characters, his language is highly, sometimes exaggeratedly, poetic. The only other character who, although rarely, speaks in lively, drawn-out similes is the princess, from whom we expect such speeches. An analysis of these similes would be interesting, but must be omitted here. Nobody else in the play uses similes.

Goethe wrote a number of less successful plays, including comedies, and even a continuation of Mozart's *Magic Flute*, as well as an entirely symbolic play, *Pandora* and, of course, *Faust*.

One other rather interesting play is *The Natural Daughter,* which I shall discuss in the context of Goethe's reactions to the French Revolution.

In the 1790's Goethe's interest in the theater showed itself in his activities as director of the Weimar stage, a position to which he devoted much time and energy and in which he felt supported by his friend Schiller, of whose mature plays Goethe directed the first productions. After Schiller's death he withdrew from the theater to which he had given so much of his life's work.

CHAPTER 5

Novels

I *Introductory Remarks*

GOETHE wrote three major novels. The first two were received with enthusiasm, the third with a certain critical reserve. The first novel, *The Sorrows of Young Werther*, had an overwhelming success and was immediately translated into a number of languages; but it was not nearly as often imitated as the second one, *Wilhelm Meister's Apprenticeship*, which became the model for all those later German novels that are characterized in Germany as "Bildungsromane," i.e., extended narratives concerning the development and formation of a young man, often an artist, toward growth and maturity. If the third novel, *Elective Affinities*, was imitated at all, this is not a striking feature of its history, for its public was slow in developing a real understanding of it. It is a profound work and in its insights and presentation far ahead of the time of its publication (1809).

Werther is an epistolary novel, imitating Rousseau's *Nouvelle Héloise* and many other French and English epistolary novels of the time. *Wilhelm Meister* resembles the earlier European picaresque novel and, more specifically, the English derivatives of this genre, mainly Fielding's *Tom Jones*. *Elective Affinities* by contrast is, in its formal aspects, a much more modern novel, with a tight central plot, a significant symbolic structure and the felt presence of an ironic narrator.

What I am trying to point out in these few remarks is the fact that Goethe experimented with various prose forms, and that each of his novels was the result of a particular type of experimentation. We may loosely call these forms the epistolary novel, the episodic novel of development, and the novel with a tight plot in which both letters and episodes appear rarely and when they do, are subordinated to the central plot. It follows from this fact that generalizations on Goethe's novels are necessarily oversimplified. It would even be false to speak of a clear-cut development—except perhaps in the jump from the episodic novel to the tightly knit plot of *Elective Affinities*, which Goethe must have considered as a form by far surpassing in cohesion the various types existing throughout the eighteenth century. The construction of the plot of *Elective Affinities* reminds the reader more of Henry James's novels than of Fielding's or Marivaux's. Goethe's sense of form obviously forced him to move in the direction of greater strictness and less freedom.

But we should not overlook the fact that even the *Sorrows of Young Werther* is an unusually tight novel, and that *Wilhelm Meister*, despite its episodic and seemingly rambling plot, is controlled by a knowing narrator who has the reins firmly in his hand. Goethe was at times long-winded and liked, in his later years, to insert general observations, but he was always conscious and very much in control of form.

As to the problem of "realism," which immediately comes to mind when discussing the novels of the eighteenth and earlier nineteenth centuries, Goethe's novels are a mixture of complete faithfulness to "reality" and a playing with reality for artistic reasons. Thus the author uses "realistic" objects as symbols, which then take on a meaning far beyond their literal appearance. Thus, e.g., Wilhelm Meister repeatedly encounters a little medicine bag which changes hands but which, within the novel, is a symbolic leitmotiv guiding the hero toward the beloved. All three novels abound in such symbolic signals given both to the characters and the readers.

As should be clear from what has been said so far, the techniques used in these novels are very rich. They show Goethe to have been a deft craftsman in full control of his artistic means. Details, I hope, will become clearer in the discussion of the individual novels.

II The Sorrows of Young Werther

The book was written in 1774 and became a world success almost immediately. Like Rousseau's *Nouvelle Héloise*, it corresponded to the need, on the part of the readers in the later part of the eighteenth century, to find emotions expressed directly and through imagery, rather than through conceptualization and what was then called "reason." Werther's behavior as well as his language are characterized by the immediacy of emotional expression, which derived its primary motivation from a lively reaction against the enlightenment and the dictates of Aristotle's *Poetics*. This reaction was fostered not only by Rousseau, but also by Shaftesbury's thoughts on enthusiasm and many related ideas showing man as a being governed by feelings rather than rational intents and purposes.

What made the book so popular is the conciseness and general excellence with which a "sentimental" (*empfindsamer*) hero is portrayed. The modern reader may not, on first reading, be quite as attracted to it as were the "sentimental" readers of the late eighteenth century. For our mode of expression runs neither as high nor as low as Goethe's, nor do our "heroes" seem to be quite as idle, self-centered and singleminded. However, such an immediate response to the work would be uncritical: we are not dealing with a "sentimental" work, but rather with a beautifully constructed novel which deliberately presents the tragedy of a sentimental hero in a nonsentimental mode. It is not the author, but his character, Werther, who is sentimental. A conscious poetic distance is observed throughout the work, which has to be realized before the novel can be appreciated as the truly great work it is.

Although the book is couched in the form of personal letters written by Werther to his friend Wilhelm, who is not expected to reply, it has an objective framework. It begins with an "accompanying letter," i.e., some authorial remarks with which the narrator disengages himself from the hero. He clearly does not intend to pour out his own heart. Addressing his readers, he says of Werther: "You cannot withhold your admiration and love from his mind and character, nor your tears from his fate." More important perhaps is the end of the novel. From May 4 of the first year to December 17 of the second year spanned by the action of the novel, the book is written in the form of carefully dated letters, all of them written by Werther himself. After the latter date, a new mode of expression is used, entitled "The Editor to the Reader." A few more letters by Werther are included in this final part: one, dated December 20, to his friend Wilhelm (to whom most previous letters are addressed), and two undated ones to Lotte, his beloved. The second of these is written "after 11 P.M.," immediately preceding Werther's suicide. A few brief notes written by Werther are found after his death and quoted in the concluding part. But the remainder of this portion is a report on Werther's last days which, as the "editor" says, he collected from the various witnesses linked to the unfortunate hero. This report is written without a trace of sentimentality. In fact, the last lines of the last paragraph have that kind of monumental simplicity and objectivity of which only a perfectly self-disciplined writer is capable:

The presence of the "Amtmann" (Lotte's father) and his arrangements attracted a crowd. At 11 P.M. he had him buried at the spot Werther had chosen. The old man and his sons followed the casket. Albert (Lotte's husband) was unable to do anything. They feared for Lotte's life. Artisans carried him. No priest accompanied him.

This is the end of the work, and its laconic tone and short sentences affect us more strongly than Werther's own emotional outbursts. It is the contrast between the "editor's" and Werther's style which most forcefully indicates the aesthetic distance.

One might add one more observation on the remarkable control with which the emotional outbursts of the hero are recorded. There is never a line where the reader feels that the book has run away with its author. On the contrary, both the length and the depth of these outbursts are carefully controlled by an author who does not identify himself with the writer of the letters. This, too, could be shown in detail by analyzing any one of Werther's letters. They are beautifully balanced and written with the attention span of a reader in mind. There are none of the asides or psychological detours which are characteristic of such authors as Sterne or even Rousseau. Every word in the book is entirely to the point.

Looking at the structure of the work as a whole—with the exclusion of the words of the "editor" at the end—we do not find it to be symmetrically arranged. Part One spanning the period from May to October of the first year, is much longer than Part Two, although the latter covers fifteen months. This is as it should be, because in the first few months Werther's tragic love for Lotte, who at that time is engaged but not yet married to Albert, begins and develops. In the very first letters, the reader is acquainted with the hero before he meets Lotte; then there is an almost three weeks' pause in the correspondence

(May 27-June 16) during which he meets her. Albert arrives on July 30, and one month later (September 3) Werther decides to leave the town. The events of that summer are the cause of both his happiness and his downfall.

Werther passes a long winter, described in just a few pages, at the court of some prince, travels for a short time and returns to Lotte after her marriage, sometime in July of the following year. The letters written between that time and December 17 are short and contain practically none of the rich descriptions offered during the first few months. All this amounts to a concise rendering of the tragic development of Werther's heart and reflects the rich profusion of his mind during the first blissful shock of meeting Lotte, and his later poverty of mind, of which he complains bitterly when he realizes that she is lost to him.

Just as the length or shortness of his letters is indicative of the situation of his heart, so are the secondary events and characters in the story, above all the seasons. Werther falls in love in the spring, is happy for a while during the summer, leaves in the fall, lives as an "exile" during the winter, returns in the summer and dies the day before Christmas. Nor is anything else in the work irrelevant or merely decorative. The time-structure is only one example of the artistic relevance of each detail.

Since Goethe did not consider nature, i.e., man's environment, as being always beneficial or "good," he could use it, in many of his prose works, as the reflection of man's changing emotions. The examples in *Werther* are particularly rich. The little town in which the hero meets Lotte strikes him as unpleasant, but the surrounding nature is in its glory and becomes his real home; many of his happiest encounters with Lotte take place in nature. However, these same places become terrifying during his second stay. On September 15 of the second year, he writes desperately about some beautiful old nut-trees, once belonging to a minister they had visited together and cut down after his death by the wife of his successor. And on December 8 he describes the wild floods which sweep over the places where they had been sitting or walking together, including his beloved Walheim (i.e., "home of his choosing") where he had hoped to settle and be happy.

The same interesting technique [2] is used in Werther's meetings with secondary, and apparently irrelevant, characters. Some of them appear twice, first happily and later unhappily situated.

Some appear only once, as the girls at the well in the beginning, or the unhappy madman toward the end. They all serve the same function: they reflect Werther's or Lotte's situation and, by reflecting it, enhance its significance. Thus a young woman mentioned in the letter of May 27 anticipates his first meeting with Lotte.

The same is true for every character and event, for example, for the books read by Werther or Lotte. A happy Werther reads Homer in the beginning, overemphasizing no doubt his "idyllic" qualities. An unhappy Werther is reading Ossian toward the end, and it matters little that the long, gloomy quotations from Ossian were not actually written by Ossian.[3] After Werther's death, Lessing's *Emilia Galotti* is found open, obviously the last thing Werther read; again it was read for its general mood rather than for Emilia's death which resembles Werther's very little.[4] Even the pantheistic remarks made by Werther in the beginning fall into this pattern of mood-creating reflections. He is a pantheist only as long as his heart overflows; but he loses his pantheistic mood—there is no better term—when he loses his happiness.

In discussing the protagonist of this novel, we must be careful to separate his actual behavior from his self-interpretations. But it is striking to note that Werther is a very acute and critical observer of himself and can almost always be completely trusted. At the beginning of the book we find a few hints concerning Werther's decision to leave his hometown and the reason for his selection of the town he finds himself in. He had some love-trouble at home which made him wish to leave. Also, during his stay at the court, he has to take care of an inheritance withheld from his mother. But these motivations remain external and do not influence the plot. However, his sudden presence in a lovely region during springtime is decisive for his future. Werther seems content, so happy in fact that he stops painting, which must have been his main previous occupation. Obviously wealthy enough to live without work or care, he is completely idle and ready to observe the beauty of the place. He does not even want his friend to send him his books (May 13): "I do not want to be guided, encouraged or inspired any more, since my heart flows over of its own accord."

He has a rich imagination and wants to limit his reading to Homer. Whenever "he returns into himself he finds a world." His serene introspection is tempered by his acute observation of nature and by the little events he reports—whose sinister meanings he can, of course, not understand. Compared with Faust, he is more contemplative and happier in his idleness than the latter is in his activities. In a very selective way, Werther's mind is open to simple and, as he calls them, "natural" events and characters, a tendency which is enhanced and instructed, as it were, by his reading of Homer. His present life is idyllic, and his mind is open only to idyllic scenes. It is the observation of such an idyl—namely Lotte surrounded by her younger brothers and sisters, for whom she is cutting bread—which causes him to fall in love with her. Had he found her in a less "natural" situation, he might never have noticed her. Obviously, a good deal of education of which he is quite unaware, enters into this apparent simplicity.

We have reached here, very quickly, the limits of the idyllic life, if it is led by a young man who, although theoretically attracted to it, does not find it to be congenial. As Werther describes himself a little later, he is actually neither serene nor calm, but restless and easily thrown about by the events of life. During the few weeks of his idyllic life with Lotte, he seems to have become oblivious to his own past or even his own character, and he indulges in an idyllic perfection for which he will ultimately have to pay with his life. Over these first weeks there falls no shadow, no fear of Albert's coming, and no remorse for feeling happy with another man's betrothed. Werther plunges into the idyl without self-restraint or even self-consciousness. His emotion has completely swept him off his feet, and there is not a trace of rationality, practicality or so-called realism left—until Albert enters the scene. It is the total abandonment to his emotion which makes Werther so disturbing to the reader. No struggle, no attempt to control his love, no sense of responsibility —all these terms are phantoms in the presence of his sweeping emotion. The only restraint comes from his "natural" respect for the woman he loves—to a large extent this is a platonic love (see letter of July 16), a love satisfied with the contemplation of the perfection of its object. Only shortly before the end of the novel does Werther become physically jealous of Albert's prerogatives. But in the glory of his first love he is almost excessively chaste. This is probably the reason why Lotte reacts so openly and unsuspiciously. She is swept along by his enthusiasm and, although a good deal less romantic and more realistic than he, lets herself be carried away almost in the same unconscious stream of happiness which carries him.[5]

The sudden end of these happy weeks does not disturb Werther more than was to be expected, and he is rather quickly prepared to leave the town. Goethe could have omitted Werther's winter at the court and placed the events of the following winter at the end of the first year. However, by stretching out the time-span he gained several advantages: he shows Werther's honest attempt to overcome his love and, at the same time, the depth of the wound inflicted. He also shows the nice contrast between the shallow life at the court and the previous "heart-filled" life in nature. During his court-period, Werther writes, quite realistically, a few letters to Lotte and Albert, but, by and large, it is again Wilhelm who receives the reports on the state of his heart. Once Werther returns to Lotte, the outcome becomes more and more inevitable. It is frightening to witness the extent to which he draws Lotte with him and destroys her happiness and Albert's. He becomes very quickly his worst self, and only now do we realize how much his self-centered emotion has harmed not only himself, but those around him. All this is very carefully developed —and not until Werther's last visit to Lotte (told in the third person) is there a mutual and passionate declaration of love. But even then it is not guilt (see letter of November 3rd) that drives Werther to commit suicide, although he mentions "sin"—rather contemptuously—in his last letter to Lotte. It is more correct to say that his emotion has been inverted: What, in the beginning, seemed a drive toward love, happiness, nature, and vitality, has now turned against him. He has been driven against himself because he could not have what his heart needed—nothing less would do. His is not a character which, through resignation and a powerful will, can grow to maturity.

On a more philsophical level, the idea of suicide was, from the beginning, included in his emotional pantheism. Allusions to suicide, never considered sinful in this context, are frequent from the very beginning. However, although he prepares it carefully and in an "orderly manner," the desperate suicide Werther actually commits is not the kind he contemplated in the beginning as a way that would take him directly to the fountainhead of all life. Long ago he has lost touch with the enthusiastic pantheism which his life in nature had inspired in him. He kills himself in emptiness, not in fullness, and in an emotional disturbance caused by his knowledge both of Lotte's love and of her permanent loss.

No other character in the novel is seen from the inside. Even Lotte's emotions are hardly in evidence. While she enjoys being with Werther, she never forgets her fiancé and marries him without apparent qualms. That she, too, loves Werther is made evident only at the very end of the work.

Technically speaking, the treatment of Lotte offers a good solution. The book is, after all, an epistolary novel. Only the writer of the letters—and there is only one, since the novel does not contain a correspondence—can truly be known from within. He is the person who expresses his feelings and his despairs, while everyone else is only seen from his subjective point of view. Werther's letters are not love-letters, since they are addressed to a friend, whose answers we never see; but they are directed to someone who never seems to tire of listening to the protagonist's personal outpourings. In this fiction, so well maintained by the author, no one except Werther himself is truly speaking about his thoughts and feelings. Even if he reports a conversation with Lotte faithfully, his is still the reporting mind. Perhaps she appears so untouched by the events because we view her reactions only through the eyes of her admirer, who is quite blind to her predicament. The fiction of the one-way letters is all the more credible since Werther does not know, or care to know, what really goes on in her mind and heart. Only when the personal letters stop, toward the end, do we learn something about Lotte's true situation.

The same applies to the character of Albert, whom Werther simply ignores. He holds him in contempt and never asks about his feelings or even prerogatives. Nor does he worry about Lotte's feelings for her husband, which he considers nonexistent. Werther's egocentricity in all these important matters knows no bounds. While he knows himself well, as was stated before, he has no knowledge of others or the desire to know them. The shockingly self-centered quality of his emotions is the inevitable concomitant of a person highly preoccupied with analyzing his own emotions, but incapable of "understanding." A similar statement can be made about most of Goethe's male characters, whereas it is not true for the female ones, who seem to be expected, by the author, to "understand" his male egomaniacs. That, to a certain point, Goethe must be identified with his characters is undeniable. But in all his own crises, as they are reflected in his works, he lets his characters perish, whereas the author himself survived. As we have seen earlier, Goethe had a great gift of freeing himself from pain or guilt by presenting it in a work of literature. In the work of art he was able to carry to a consistent conclusion the events of his life which in reality were, as are most of our experiences, imperfect and half-hearted.[6]

III Wilhelm Meister's Lehrjahre

Published after twenty years of intermittent work, this novel differs from all other works of Goethe, with the exception of *Faust*, in presenting the reader with a bewildering wealth not only of characters and plot, but also of social groups, ideas, and even of narrative techniques. Yet, the whole is completely mastered, all threads are taken up, all characters and events accounted for in eight relatively short books. If the pace seems rambling, the plot is carefully planned. The unity of the work, however, is not easy to define. I will proceed by discussing first some of the innumerable problems, events, characters, and ideas, and by offering, in the end, some suggestions concerning the unity, and perhaps the meaning, of the whole.

During the long years in which Goethe sporadically worked on the novel, the emphasis changed together with his outlook on life. Since we have the earliest version,[7] unpublished at the time, we know that in it Wilhelm frees himself from his bourgeois, mercantile environment and hopes to find real freedom on the stage. Gradually, as Goethe matured, he began to discover the comparatively empty life of actors and, already before he completed the work under the influence of Schiller (1794–6), he had introduced an entirely new group of characters nonexistent in his earlier plan: the members of the so-called *Turmgesellschaft* (The Society of the Tower), which became more and more influential as the work proceeded. This fact, biographical in nature, changes the outlook and meaning of the entire novel.

I would also like to introduce an historical consideration, equally intended to further the understanding of the work. *Wilhelm Meister's Apprenticeship* is eminently a novel of the eighteenth century. It sums up, and in certain ways surpasses in scope and meaning, such earlier novels as *Tom Jones*, Lesage's *Gil Blas* and many others. Yet it remains a modified adventure novel. And while Goethe suppresses some of the bawdiness of the earlier picaresque novel, the fundamental episodic treatment stems from there. The hero gets himself into situations, deliberately or accidentally, which, one after the other, turn out to be precarious and from which, sooner or later, he will have to extricate himself. He stumbles from one predicament to the next and continues to do so, even in the last book in which he gets himself engaged to the wrong woman. All of this is typical of the eighteenth-century successors of the picaresque novel. Equally typical of that kind of novel is the fact that the hero meets characters from all strata of society, and that these occasions are used to poke fun at, or satirize, many social groups.

Quite another kind of eighteenth-century tradition is represented by the Abbé, the moving force behind the *Turmgesellschaft*. His ideas are those of the enlightenment; he is worldly, tolerant, and by inclination an educator. For him, Wilhelm, with his naive understanding of art and life, is the ideal target for educational experiments. The Abbé had also educated, more or less successfully (but always with a good deal of insight), the entire *Turmgesellschaft*, of whose principal members he had been the official tutor.

It is around him that the society had first gathered as a kind of masonic lodge—another eighteenth-century feature. The masonic ideals will, more or less, be upheld when the members become adults, but the ritual and symbolism is subsequently taken with a grain of salt. Nevertheless, the society continues to work with a common goal in mind, which, as time goes by, becomes more important to them than the ritual—namely to prepare themselves for a new type of society to be founded in the New World.

In the midst of this *Turmgesellschaft* there are, furthermore, members—some of them taken seriously, others openly ridiculed— who are connected with pietistic groups and societies. It need hardly be mentioned to what an extent pietism was a feature of the educated German society in the second half of the eighteenth century.

Both the treatment of the whole work in the manner of earlier travel literature and the individual features just enumerated have a distinct eighteenth-century flavor. Nevertheless, the work was greeted by the young Friedrich Schlegel [8] as the ideal representative of the new "romantic novel." The reasons for this praise will have to be discussed later.

German critics generally consider the work to be what in German is called a *Bildungsroman* or novel of education. A better meaning, in Goethe's own sense of "Bildung," would be novel of formation or novel of development. Whereas, with very few exceptions, the educational efforts are of a questionable nature,— sometimes they simply amount to tricks—there is no doubt that the entire work is meant to present to the reader a naive young man who, through his varied experiences, grows to be a man. At the end of the novel, the reader has gained some, although not much, confidence that Wilhelm might one day become what his name indicates, a master.

Goethe likes to compare a man's growth to that of a tree. And while this favorite metaphor of his indicates the limitations which lie in the fact that nobody can grow into anything other than what is given to him in the pattern of his seed, the image also implies that, if the growing tree is given its rightful place under the sun, it will grow into the perfection of this pattern. "Bildung," taken in this particular sense, is very much what Goethe had in mind when he wrote the novel. He gives his hero a vast realm of experience, which allows him to grow more freely than almost any other novelistic hero. Wilhelm can amble through his early years, without any responsibility, always mysteriously provided with money and protected, even without his knowing it, by the distant *Turmgesellschaft*, which suddenly makes its presence felt when he is in a particularly bad situation.

In accordance with the metaphor of the tree, Goethe has endowed his hero with a number of features which remain constant throughout the work. Wilhelm is impressionable, often somewhat bland, happily aimless and pompous almost as soon as he opens his mouth. He is rash in his judgment, temperamental, and easily thrown into enthusiasm or despair. With the exception perhaps of the aimlessness, most of these features remain with him to the end and it would be wrong to say that he learns to control his emotions. Rather, the very opposite is true. Wilhelm continues to err, to be desperate about his errors and to find himself unexpectedly, and often painfully, relieved of a mistaken or misjudged situation. Similarly, his judgment of characters and events is often erroneous. This, too, remains true throughout the novel. Goethe carefully and skillfully avoids bestowing on his hero a steady growth, either in character or in insight and judgment, and it can thus be said with much justification that Wilhelm "learns" very little. Unless, therefore, the term *Bildungsroman* is taken to mean nothing other than the opportunity given to a character to grow in his own way and at his own speed and inner laws, the term is barely applicable to *Wilhelm Meister*.

It is, however, wrong to say that Wilhelm's function in the work is simply that of a young man who must grow and develop. His activities are by no means all of a receptive nature. In fact, there is a great deal of mutual interaction between him and almost all the other characters. This give-and-take is an important part of the work, and while some of the characters try very hard to be Wilhelm's "educators," most are quite unaware of their particular educational function and some are simply recipients of Wilhelm's good will and nature. They are also, directly or indirectly, educated by Wilhelm, and it is even more important and, probably decisive, for the interest which the novel holds, that most of Wilhelm's relationships are those of love and friendship, of mutual interest and assistance. In many instances, the educational value for Wilhelm seems quite incidental. In other words, conscious education forms only a small segment of Wilhelm's progress of development, which is often greatly advanced by the "accidents" of life—which, to be sure, are placed so carefully by the author as to produce some such development.

Connected with this mutual interaction is Wilhelm's eagerness to listen to the stories told him by the people he encounters. It is perhaps his greatest talent to be an excellent listener, which elicits in each character his or her essential story; and the novel is woven around this interaction of telling and listening. It should also be taken into account that his young life has been rather protected and is, in itself, uninteresting. Wilhelm has few stories of his own to tell. His only interesting experience, his affair with Marianne, is never mentioned to anyone until the end of the work when he is confronted with his and Marianne's son and her old servant. At his young age, he is not a fascinating character, and without the richness of the life around him, there would be no novel.

To be sure, it could be argued that listening rather than speaking is symptomatic of the educational process. But Wilhelm's listening is of a peculiar quality. He does not listen in order to record what he hears, but rather out of a warm and sympathetic heart. He acts and reacts to the tales he hears and becomes involved with the persons and their situations—in other words, he acts like a warm and interested human being, not as the object of a very subtle educational intent. He may be an uninteresting character and his blandness may never quite leave him—but he is nevertheless a rounded human being, in whose sympathetic interest many more colorful and original characters are mirrored. This essential role of Wilhelm as a solicitor of other characters' past or present difficulties, born out of a gentle and interested sympathy and real human warmth, adds much to the artistic quality of the work.

From the inception of the novel, Wilhelm Meister's life was planned to take place in strata of society, very different from his own, which he either chooses or into which he is accidentally thrown. At times, the various groups to which he attaches himself seem almost more important to the author than is the hero himself, and the question whether this is a "social" novel or a novel centering around one individual can hardly be avoided. Indeed, we learn much about the status of actors, their various companies, their problems and their predicaments. We also learn about the bourgeois society from which Wilhelm successfully escapes, and which he despises. And we finally learn about some of the aristocracy's ambitious desires and serious activities.

None of these groups, however, is described with a view toward social change. Goethe is not, in that sense, a social critic. What interests him throughout is the individual rather than the group; i.e., the specific character as he behaves and moves within his particular sphere. Goethe never displays a reformer's zeal. One example may serve for many: Wilhelm is ultimately drawn toward the aristocracy. One of the reasons for this attraction is their more refined behavior which is strongly contrasted with the rude, greedy, temperamental manners of the actors. Nowhere does Goethe attempt to excuse the actor's behavior, to understand it from a sociological point of view or to wish to change their social conditions. Satire or social criticism, although always present, were obviously not Goethe's main concern.

He looks, rather, at society with the eyes of an observer of nature. You cannot be sympathetic or antipathetic toward the forces of evolution because they simply exist. No sympathy will change the laws of nature, and Goethe knew this only too well. For him, society was no more arbitrary than nature, and he accepted its stratifications with the same indifference with which he accepted the laws of nature. What prevented him from being a social reformer was his acceptance of everything that exists, be it in nature or society. In these fundamental questions, Goethe did not distinguish, as do most modern thinkers as well as the eighteenth-century satirists, between what nature made and what man made. And it did not occur to him to use a novel, meant to present human beings as individuals, as a vehicle to fight social injustice. This is clearly not the purpose of his book.

Social distinctions, while well portrayed, actually play a minor role in the novel. The class lines, although clearly drawn, are constantly crossed by many of the characters. Wilhelm, a bourgeois by birth, is freely accepted, first by the actors who take advantage of him, and later by the *Turmgesellschaft* which, in its desire for useful activity, moves almost in the direction of the bourgeoisie. In the end, the light-minded actress Philine is graciously allowed to marry into the *Turmgesellschaft*, whereas Friedrich, her aristocratic lover, behaves more like a carefree and eccentric adventurer. Ultimately, the social strata, although acknowledged as existing, are treated in a remarkably unorthodox way. The novel shows how readily the lines separating the classes can be crossed and is probably a rather faithful portrayal of late eighteenth-century society in its transition from aristocratic rule to bourgeois dominance.

Goethe's interest in the individual character is not concentrated on the hero alone. Within his prose-works the characters of this novel occupy a very special place. They are truly individuals, vibrant with life and personality. According to their role in the novel, they are treated with light irony, complete seriousness, banter or respect. They are in almost constant motion, free and unencumbered even if their lives are as tragic as Marianne's, Aurelie's or Mignon's. Goethe always had a special talent for presenting women whose peculiarities he observed more lovingly than those of men. The women in *Wilhelm Meister* run the gamut from wild, carefree, sorrowful, desperate to restrained, efficient, gentle and serene figures. Some of Goethe's most unforgettable female characters enliven the work. The light-hearted Philine, who first draws him into the group of actors, is probably the most attractive of these. Old women, such as the old servant of Marianne, play their part; and so do elegant women, such as the Countess, sister of Wilhelm's future wife, Natalie. Even Natalie, toward the end the image of near-perfection, appears first on horseback, interestingly disguised in her uncle's overcoat. The list is endless, and the characters vary greatly. Among the many male characters, Lotharie, the leader of the Tower society, is one of the most attractive. Having just lost his fiancee, Terese, because he once had an affair with her mother, he is a remarkable philanderer. Earlier, he had been the cause of Aurelie's despair and suicide, but he lightheartedly explains to Wilhelm, who brought him the sad news, that Aurelie was never "lovable." She and Terese have already been replaced by Lydia who is subsequently removed from the castle, where she had become a nuisance. After Lothario's recovery from a wound he has received in a duel, he immediately visits an earlier love and, finding her image rejuvenated in the figure of her niece, he is not far from toying with another love—while, all along, making inquiries to find out whether the pretended mother of Terese really was her mother—which, of course, she was not. This, in a nutshell, is the life of a man of the world, told with subtle irony. It is generally accepted, and nobody doubts Lothario's ability to be the leader of the group that plans to colonize in the budding United States.

I could have chosen any number of male characters to point out the light touch displayed by an author whom we have not always found so playful. Serenely, and with tongue-in-cheek, Goethe allows his characters to fall into traps, commit gross errors of judgment, stumble into predicaments or find themselves unexpectedly retrieved. The plot ambles along, allowing for any number of such adventures. Included in this happy game are great tragedies and profound insights into the horrors of existence. But even those tragedies are part of the game which the author plays with such great skill.

At this point of the discussion, two concepts must be introduced, both originating with Schiller. We can translate them as illusion (*Schein*) and play or playfulness (*Spiel*). In his

Briefe über ästhetische Erziehung (Letters on Aesthetic Education), written just before the time when Goethe was working on *Wilhelm Meister*, Schiller claimed that these two concepts define the essence of art. *Wilhelm Meister* exemplifies this statement to perfection. Here, an omniscient author creates the rules for the game he has proposed for himself, and he plays the game according to these self-imposed rules. All along, he smiles ironically as he creates the pitfalls for the character whom he alone can free again. The freedom which the author must feel when he plays his game is transferred to his hero, whose freedom, less absolute than the author's, is nevertheless joyously felt. Art, as Schiller understood it, does not *degenerate* into a game, but rather is *elevated* to it. The lightness of touch, and the playfulness of the author, are expressions of his supreme and free creativity and his aesthetic distance. When the young romanticist Friedrich Schlegel read the novel, he recognized this element and identified it as his own concept of irony which, for him, was an expression of that freedom and that distance with regard to his subject matter.

Schiller's concept of illusion is perhaps even more far-reaching in its implications. Goethe has an almost uncanny talent for producing illusions which do not correspond to reality. Over and over again he shows how easily we are deceived by our senses. This starts in the first book when Wilhelm sees a man leaving Marianne's house. He feels immediately deceived by her and breaks with her forever. Little does he realize that Marianne had rejected this man, a former lover, and was faithfully and proudly waiting for Wilhelm. Long after her lonely death, Wilhelm is told the story, to his heart's despair.

Wilhelm Meister is crowded with mistaken identities, disguises and many other optical or intellectual delusions. Some have been mentioned here, such as the "amazon" disguised in her uncle's coat. There is also the comic one when the Count at the castle sees in the mirror what he believes to be his own image in nightcap and housecoat and is immediately converted to pietism, without bothering to find out that, in reality, his double was Wilhelm disguised as the Count for a tryst with the Countess.

Mignon, disguised as a boy, comes from nowhere. We learn her life's history only after we have observed her throughout the novel as the loyal follower of Wilhelm, who has taken a liking to her, largely because of her mysteriousness. The novel is painted in a chiaroscuro in which disguises and radical changes of personality, as well as unexpected revelations as to a character's identity, are commonplace.

The recounted portions of the novel, constituting only a small sample of the events, were selected for a specific end. While similar mystifications, transformations, etc., occur in every trivial novel of the period, what Goethe manages to achieve is to transform mystification into mystery. The mysterious sources of human passions, that intangible quality in a person which Goethe liked to call demonic, and the truly tragic events caused by the apparently light play of love—these are the mysteries Goethe is able to glean from the vast harvest of incident and character. The "amazon" appearing to the wounded young man in his hour of need, and disappearing mysteriously, will be the guiding light of his life: Mignon will, in the end, appear as an angel of light relieved from the burden of her dark and painful life. Goethe makes full use of the potential of mystification to become mysterious truth. When, shortly before her death, Mignon appears in a white dress, she sings the following song: "Oh let me *seem* until I will *be*." [9]

For her, this last disguise (her appearance as an angel) is an indication of what she will be only after death. Her lines, however, sum up everyone's need for disguises. No figure in the novel is ever what he might potentially be. Everyone wears his disguises, mystifies others, and appears, at times enigmatic. The core of the personality, the "entelechy," develops very slowly under many masks, whose gradual removal might lead to a true understanding of the person.

That this is the purpose of the work as it stands seems also evident from the presence of the theater which, by definition, is the place of illusions. Goethe contrasts, rather impressively, the actual personalities of the actors with their role on the stage. On the stage, they are elevated to the level of their roles, whereas in actual life they are petty, greedy, and quarrelsome. Art, in this context, seems like a benign curtain covering up the dreary reality.

What Jarno, a member of the Tower group, reproaches Wilhelm's performance of Hamlet with, is the fact that Wilhelm, in playing Hamlet, played only himself. The uncertain, undecided Hamlet on whom action is forced against his wishes was certainly one of the inspirations from which the young Goethe drew. In our context, this means that, in acting Hamlet, Wilhelm does not do what a good actor should do, namely conceal himself and fashion the stage character from the dramatic material. To be oneself on the stage is artistically wrong and contradicts, besides, the meaning of the novel, in which revelations of personality are slow in coming and "disguises" are much closer to the essence of human relationships, even if they are misconceptions. In revealing himself on the stage, Wilhelm is certainly not a good actor.

In this context, we have to come back to Schiller's Essay on Aesthetic Education. From the beginning the Abbé makes an effort to educate Wilhelm toward a truer understanding of the essence of art. The only intellectual education Wilhelm ever receives, the place in his mind which is clearly shown to be in need of improvement, is his aesthetic judgment. In the first book, Wilhelm tells the stranger—who subsequently turns out to be the Abbé in disguise—how much he loved the picture of a sick prince in his grandfather's art collection because of the sentimental feelings it evoked in him. Throughout the work, one or another member of the *Turm* tries to teach him an aesthetic attitude which looks dispassionately at the content of art and is fascinated with its formal appearance. There are many hints which make it clear that our sensitive hero understands none of this. Even in the end, when he finds his beloved picture of the sick prince in Natalie's home, we cannot be sure that this aesthetic education has been effective. But the *Turmgesellschaft* has done its best to instill in Wilhelm Schiller's dearest ideal.

Nobody can deny that the *Turmgesellschaft* is a more appropriate company for Wilhelm than the actors. Their common goal, namely the founding of an ideal society in a new country, similar to the one envisaged in the *Märchen*,[10] is based on the idea of the complete cooperation of all its members, for each of whom a place will be assigned according to his own talents and personality. In that respect, they are much superior to the actors, whose common goal, namely a perfect performance, is certainly not attained by discipline and well organized cooperation.

But it seems wrong to overemphasize the superiority of the *Turmgesellschaft*. In the first place, its members are by no means ready for their goal and seem, in fact, far from approaching it. They are dispersed, going their own, often erroneous, ways.

Being wrong, choosing the wrong path, and getting into the wrong situations, is as characteristic of them, as it is of anyone else in the work. In fact, the unity of the entire novel consists in this essential feature, without which, as Goethe makes very clear, no insight can be gained. Even the "Schöne Seele," (Book VI), the aunt of the Tower-group, is included in this treatment— for her life is not different from that of anyone else. She, too, errs and has to retrace her steps more than once. In order to find some vague quietistic peace, she has to go through much of "life" with its vicissitudes and uncertainties. She, too, is in almost constant motion, both physically and emotionally. If there is one truly quiet character, it is Natalie, who is not, like most of the others, restless, but instead quietly active. She has that inner balance which Wilhelm lacks and admires. But in comparison with all the other colorful characters, she remains strangely pale —an ideal more than a human being. When Wilhelm first falls in love with her, however, she is not only disguised but in motion, fleeing from a band of robbers.

That the *Turmgesellschaft*, as a group was not meant by Goethe to represent "ideal society," is obvious from many critical remarks made either by members of the society, or, very often, by Wilhelm, who considers his *Lehrbrief* [11] e.g., at least in a moment of anger, to be pompously inane. Friedrich mocks the whole group, and none of the members has kept his earlier belief in the importance of the rituals and secret signs. At moments Goethe actually treats them ludicrously, as when the Ghost in *Hamlet* is furnished by them—in itself a ludicrous episode—and turns out to be the Abbé's twin brother, whose only appearance in the work this is. Even the Abbé's various disguises show little dignity. Quite often Goethe "uses" the society to bring together the disparate parts of his plot; and in this respect he does not treat them differently from the less elevated characters.

Unless one counts the *Turmgesellschaft* as part of the game which the author is playing, one cannot do justice to the novel. The lightness of treatment and the gentle irony prevail even here, and Wilhelm is by no means guided by a group of lifeless ideals.

It may be important to realize that, except for Aurelie, who is also linked with the group through Lothario, every death that occurs or is related takes place in their realm. And while death is very clearly interpreted as a part and a reminder of life, it is nevertheless a stark reality which points at the limitations of man's activities. And while, toward the end, restlessness and pure motion turn into disciplined activity, we also hear, at that point in the novel, the chaotic story of the harp-player and Mignon. The aristocratic group has, to be sure, a larger scope than do the actors—they embrace a larger realm of active life. But they also embrace death and the dark side of life. Wilhelm's acquaintance with the Tower Society is thus a complex one. Whereas he learned to "live" and love from the actors, here he meets with the profounder problems of life. Harmony is not so much the answer to this new situation as is maturity. As the work ends, Wilhelm is happy in the hope of marrying Natalie. But we know from the *Wanderjahre* that he will always be separated from her. In some dark way, maturing is a process undergone by the isolated individual. Goethe clearly undercut any superficial harmony by inserting stories of death and insanity, or prospects of loneliness and struggle. The lightness of the book is felt less often toward the end, as deeper chords are struck. Far from ending in harmony, then, the novel opens the abysses of life and leaves Wilhelm standing at their edge.

But this must not be seen as presupposing a pessimistic outlook. Just as Mignon and the Harpist are woven into the book very early, so Friedrich appears at the end, gay as ever, to marry off Wilhelm and Natalie. What really happens is that Wilhelm's befuddled mind slowly becomes receptive not only to the world of the stage, but also to that of life and death. The novel would not encompass the fullness of life if it did not include unhappiness and misery. What Wilhelm learns in the presence of the society is an openness to death—and this lesson is driven home very strongly. And as he understands death, life is given to him in the person of his and Marianne's son. Only now is the life-cycle completed and Goethe can dismiss the favorite child of his imagination.

IV The Elective Affinities

Originally planned as a novella within the framework of *Wilhelm Meister's Years of Wandering*, the work was enlarged by Goethe to a full-length novel because the theme was too weighty for the comparatively narrow form of the shorter genre. Goethe was almost sixty years old when he wrote it, and had acquired a vast range in viewpoint as well as style. If the reader should be disturbed by the many generalizations, by inserted stories and diaries and by the observations on natural phenomena, he should also be aware of the tightly knit plot in which these digressions have a clear and symbolic place. Despite their existence in the novel, the tragic plot runs its course with the inevitablity of ancient tragedy.

The title of the work itself indicates this technique of an apparent digression which, in reality, is symbolic of the entire work. Eduard, "a baron in the best years of his life," his wife Charlotte and his friend, the Captain, sit together. The two men explain to Charlotte a phenomenon arising from the combination of two compound chemical substances, which, upon contact, immediately separate into their original elements and form a new chemical union with one of the elements of the other compound. The application of the phenomenon to human situations is immediately made, but the reader is left in the dark as to what new human combinations might be formed in this circle of friends. Charlotte comments that the term "elective affinities" has little to do with what really happens during the chemical process and what she considers, quite correctly, to be a "necessity of nature" rather than a free choice. The latter, she claims, lies only in the hands of the chemist who is free to bring the compounds together and thus force them to separate and reunite in a different way. In the interpretation of Goethe's work, the reader has to keep the chemical image in mind and, although Goethe called the work *Elective Affinities*, such affinities in human relations, as well as in nature, are, in his opinion, grounded in and determined by a "necessity of nature" rather than a freedom of choice. How well the image expresses the human situation is understood only much later when Charlotte's young foster-child, Ottilie, joins the three, and Eduard falls in love with her while Charlotte is strongly attracted to the Captain. The image, then, indicates the powerful nature of the love which rapidly develops between Eduard and Ottilie, and which has the inevitability of a natural disaster. For a discussion of the question of where Goethe stood in the conflict between marriage and love, as presented in the novel, the chemical image gives the only viable answer. Goethe does not advocate either marriage or adultery. Like a scientist, he observes and describes the newly developing human bonds as if they were natural phenomena, and he honestly presents what happens when affinities develop in a precarious situation.

That the marriage between Eduard and Charlotte has a "conventional," rather than an emotional, origin is clear from the beginning. The two had loved each other in their youth, but each had married another and less desirable spouse. Both spouses having died, Eduard and Charlotte found themselves free to marry each other. So they "decided" to get married and "planned" their way of life. They were not "driven" together by a strong passion, but rather united by the memory of their youth, which for neither of them contains the emotion they once experienced. The conventionality, however, lies much deeper than in their immediate plans—which always strike the reader as being more those of Charlotte than of Eduard, who is temperamentally incapable of planning. It makes itself felt in the arbitrary ways in which they have organized their new life. Eduard has laid out a large garden, carefully planned with the gardener, but later abandoned. Charlotte has built the moss hut in which the early conversations take place and which will, in the course of the story, be abandoned for the sake of the much bolder, freer "Lusthaus" for whose location Ottilie is responsible.[12]

Throughout the work, Charlotte tries to save the marriage, even when it is no longer an honest relationship. Her mind thinks in terms of marriage, and she is ready for divorce only after the central catastrophe has befallen her and her decision comes too late. As a lady of the world, she is conservative and not open to change. If she were less wealthy and leisurely, one might be tempted to call her bourgeois. Her planned and organized way of life is never completely shattered and withstands all the tragic events of the novel. From her point of view, these tragic events could have been avoided if Eduard had heeded her early warning not to let anyone, including the Captain, share their life.

But her point of view is not Goethe's. After the four characters have become aware of their own change of affections, as well as those of their partners, Charlotte, in her reasonable and virtuous manner of thinking, hopes that, with the removal of the Captain and Ottilie, "everything would be as it had been a few months previously, perhaps even much better." She hopes to restore her relationship to Eduard "very soon" and keeps "strengthening her delusion that a disturbed situation can be restored to its earlier tranquillity—that what has been violently released can be suppressed again." (Mayer, p. 106–7). This passage shows strikingly that the narrator has an infinitely more profound insight into the real forces at work than does Charlotte. What makes the novel great is not Charlotte's reasonable behavior but the irrational power of passion which seizes the two lovers.

The problematic quality of marriage in general is discussed a little earlier during the visit of the Count and the Baroness.[13] Throughout this very revealing conversation, Charlotte tries in vain to change the topic, which returns to marriage because the two guests have marriage uppermost in their minds. Both married, they had fallen in love, but while the Baroness was able to get a divorce, the Count was not. Seen from the point of view of the sacred nature of marriage, their free way of life might seem to be a symbol of the lawlessness of passion. But the book does not bear out this point of view. While their free relationship leads to an unusual case of adultery, as we shall see, they themselves are described as dignified and serene, and their remarks on marriage coincide very much with Goethe's own thoughts on the subject. The Count blames the "eternity of marriage" for some of its defects. He feels that everything else in life, in contrast to marriage, has great mobility, and he suggests that only third marriages should be considered permanently binding. In fact, Ottilie would be Eduard's third wife.

The main reason for the appearance of the Count and the Baroness in this household à quatre, which, as the Baroness quickly notices, is already underminded by passion, is the remarkable contrast they present to the central tragedy. Their love, although hampered by their respective spouses, is far from tragic. It is fulfilled, accepted and handled without a sense of guilt.

Guilt, however, although in unexpected ways, is precisely the cause of Eduard and Ottilie's tragedy. Always attracted by "unusual occurrences," Goethe had found the core of a fascinating problem: on the evening of their visit, the Count asks Eduard to show him to the Baroness's bedroom. On the way back, Eduard, deeply in love with Ottilie, stops at his wife's bedroom and makes love to her just when she had realized that she loves the Captain. No explanation is given by the reticent author. But the legitimate embrace of the couple becomes adulterous as each thinks of his real love, and the next morning they meet their heart's mates with a "sense of guilt." The result of this night is a child with the features of the Captain and Ottilie's eyes. It is the presence of the child which will make it impossible for Eduard to claim Ottilie as his wife, and it is the death of the child through Ottilie's fault which makes it impossible for her to marry Eduard.

Thus, Eduard's nocturnal visit to his wife is, in an intricate way, the basis for everyone's assessment of his feelings. When Goethe felt it necessary to enlarge the novella into a full novel, he superimposed on this "event" the idea of the elective affinities. And while Goethe was artistically successful in combining this symbolic image with the "unusual event," he greatly complicated the moral questions which the reader is bound to ask.

No adultery is actually committed aside from this strange "legitimate" one. But feelings have gone the way the "affinities" urge them to go. Charlotte and the Captain make a free decision to renounce each other, and they have every reason not to feel any guilt, at least from a conventional point of view. Eduard could well be considered the most guilty person, not only because he forsakes his wife, but also because he never displays any wisdom or restraint. He is driven by his passion and considers it his only true life. Nothing outsides of Ottilie matters to him. When he leaves the castle just before Charlotte's pregnancy becomes known, he does so exclusively for Ottilie's safety; the condition of his departure is that Ottilie will remain with Charlotte. But while he suffers from being separated from her, he does not consider this separation the penalty he has to pay for any "guilt."

Of the four characters only Ottilie feels truly guilty, and this only after she let the child fall into the lake. Toward the end of the work, Ottilie feels intensely that to her the child's death means the revelation of her guilty passion to which, up to this moment, she had abandoned herself without any self-consciousness. She is the only character in the book who thinks in the moral terms of guilt and punishment. But even Ottilie, although she is the author's favorite character, is not his mouthpiece.

What the image of the elective affinities tells us is most truly Goethe's own answer. Once the violent "natural" forces have been allowed to take their course, they do so relentlessly. They do not

ask about guilt and punishment, but simply exist. Their victims
are driven through life, and only death can give them peace.
These forces exceed the scope of guilt. If the question can seriously be raised in the *Elective Affinities*, the guilt might well
be considered to be Charlotte's for not having understood or
recognized early enough the greater forces man may be subjected to. Her world is man-made and, hence, limited. She is
kind, generous, ladylike, but fundamentally insufficient. She
tries in vain to defend her little world against the intruding
forces, against which there is no defense.

I have placed Charlotte at the center of the discussion because
she represents all the values of married life: stability, order, a
solid and gracious life. But it is too easy to say that those who
upset this life "deserve" a tragic end.

In the first place, Ottilie is an eminently innocent young
woman. She never meditates on her situation except when she
misses Eduard after his voluntary departure. And throughout the
long winter of separation she hopefully awaits his return. The
death of the child is caused by Eduard's sudden and unexpected
return, which upsets her inner balance. Nothing but a tragic
event of this immensity could make her aware of the fact that
she may have done any wrong at all. Up to this moment, Ottilie
was young, beautiful, humble and very feminine, not a brilliant
student at school, but sensitive and open to warmth of affection.
Even in her "diaries," which Goethe inserts at the beginning of the
second part, there is not a trace of guilt feeling. The guilt breaks
in on her only after the death of the child, and it changes her
entire life. Her penitence has a grandeur of its own, and while
she cannot give up her love, she can and does renounce hope.

But even Eduard is not without greatness. While he is the
most impulsive of the four characters, the most spoiled, the most
used to getting his wishes fulfilled, and while he certainly cannot
give up his love and his hope, he lives for the longest time away
from home, lonely and in pain. He may not be able to resign himself, but he is capable of great, sustained suffering.

It might be added that Charlotte, in forming the plans for
their common life, had disregarded the fact that a character of
Eduard's vitality cannot live in prolonged idleness. When he first
suggests that they should invite the Captain, the reader is made

to feel the boredom of this active man who is reduced to an idle life in the country at much too young an age.

There is a lack of a sense of direction in the activities of these idle rich. This is accentuated after trouble has descended upon them, but it is clearly in evidence before. As Eduard works in the garden and Charlotte in the larger park, the reader cannot help but feel that all these activities are arbitrary and could be handled in many other ways. A good example is Charlotte's trail from the moss-hut upward, the plan of which she allows to be changed as soon as the Captain convinces her of a better plan. This lack of direction becomes equally clear during the building of the "Lusthaus." The two men had made the plans for it, but when Ottilie suggests a better location, they immediately follow her suggestion. The Captain and Charlotte make careful financial plans for its construction. But since they seem too slow to Eduard, he pushes the project and spends much more money. Later in the story, when the Captain decides to leave his friends, he and Charlotte also give up these financial plans and, instead, help Eduard in hurrying the construction of the "Lusthaus." Throughout the work, the reader has the uneasy feeling that one contributing factor to the tragic events is the idleness and arbitrariness of the main characters' activities. The marriage, as it was planned in isolation from human beings and with a large degree of idleness, is not founded on very solid ground.

To drive home the urgency of the plot, Goethe uses a number of interesting and original techniques. One of them is his treatment of time. The novel takes place within a time span very similar to that of *Werther*, extending from the early summer of the first year to the fall of the second. It is thus even more condensed than *Werther*, covering only the most economical time spans for the events of conception, birth, and death to take place. But it is within this over-all framework of chronological time that Goethe offers his most interesting attempts at dealing with time. His greatest concern is to present realistically the psychological time of the novel, i.e., time as it is felt by the characters involved. The pace of the novel is extremely fast when important events occur: The falling in love, the death of the child and the final tragic happenings. It is almost as if these events took place so rapidly that they occupy no time at all. The Captain, e.g., even though he is less wealthy and more accustomed to disciplined work than the others, forgets to wind his watch. "Time stood still," the narrator comments. The utter involvement of the characters in the events makes them unaware of the passing of time, and Goethe passes this sense of timelessness on to the reader. Each event is told almost breathlessly in a few pages, even a few paragraphs.

The long period of time elapsing between Eduard's departure from the castle to his return, is fully described. As soon as the long separation begins, the narrative slows down. Far from skipping the months of waiting, Goethe elaborates on them, allowing the reader to share his awareness of how long the characters felt these months to be.

The reader's reaction to these slow parts, which contain, among other delaying devices, the diaries of Ottilie, the discussions with the architect and the apprentice-teacher, and the visits of Luciane and the traveling Englishman, is quite often one of impatience. The reader is anxious to know the resolution and feels held back by the meditative quality of the narration of this interim period. It is Goethe's great merit to have penetrated deeply into the nature of time as a decisive element in the novel, and to have done it so much earlier than the well-known experiments in time of the novel of the twentieth century. He had scarcely an example to go by or to learn from because the novel was then, particularly with regard to the treatment of time, in its infancy.

Another interesting technique is the treatment of secondary characters. The number of these characters is not as small as one might expect in a plot so clearly centered around one central happening. The reason may be that the largeness of the setting was needed for the plausibility of the story. Unless a castle is populated by visitors, it does not provide a realistic setting, and in many ways Goethe goes to great lengths to be realistic. But if it is true that the nineteenth century is characterized, in its most important literary aspects, by a polarity between realism and symbolism, then certainly *Elective Affinities* is a very early example of this polarity. While the entrances and exits of the secondary characters are always carefully motivated in realistic terms, and while their occurrence and recurrence is made perfectly plausible, the characters themselves are not fully realistic; they are not, like the principal characters, rounded out personalities. Most of them have only one major characteristic, which serves a functional need in the work and beyond which the reader is not informed. And whereas each of them promotes the plot at a given moment, none of them does much more than that. Their treatment is very similar to that of the secondary characters in *Werther*—they all have a symbolic value inasmuch as they either serve as a reflection of the main action or come to bear upon it in what the author would call an accidental manner.

Next to the Count and the Baroness, the most important figure is Mittler, the middle man or mediator. The fact that, by some scholars, he has been considered to express Goethe's own ideas, led to strange aberrations of judgment which have so often been the fate of Goethe's works. In the first place, he is a grotesque figure. He speaks too loudly and very often too much. He is hasty and inconsiderate. Charlotte is not satisfied with him. She feels that his quick nature may bring about some good things, but his haste is the cause of much failure. Nobody, she feels, is more dependent on momentary prejudices—a sound judgment on her part. When she tells him that she is pregnant, he immediately believes that he is no longer needed in his role as mediator between her and her husband. Little does he know about the unfortunate circumstances under which this child was conceived.

Mittler's lack of real sensitivity becomes clear on two more occasions. The first is the christening of the child, during which he gives a long speech, insensitive to the fact that the old pastor who had just christened the baby is on the verge of dying. The second, and worse, blunder occurs during his last visit to the castle when, during his speech on the Ten Commandments with special emphasis on the Sixth ("Thou shalt not commit adultery"), Ottilie enters and, as a partial consequence of his speech, dies a few hours later.

What, then, is the role of this unfortunate man? In the case of extraordinary events, his mediating quality, applicable only to average problems, is not only ineffective but uncannily destructive. He seems to be the ironic symbol of all the attempts at reconciliation, at smoothing over difficulties, at setting things right that are beyond repair. He symbolizes all the vain efforts of the participants to reachieve happiness: on Charlotte's part, the restoration of her marriage, on Eduard's part, after his return from the war, the desire to divorce Charlotte and marry Ottilie. In the night after the child's death, Charlotte says to the Major (who has been promoted from the rank of Captain): "There are certain things on which Destiny stubbornly insists. Reason and virtue, duty and all that is sacred to us oppose them in vain. Destiny wishes something to happen which seems right to it, but not to us. And in the end Destiny will be the victor, fight against it as we may." (Mayer, p. 266) Mittler would not have been able to comprehend such an insight, which Charlotte achieves in the moment of greatest pain. There is no room for tragedy in a mind such as Mittler's.

Even more ironically, this is true for the visiting Englishman who, although unhappy enough himself, does not realize what agonies of the heart the story he tells to the women creates. The lack of sensitivity with which he pursues his story is surpassed only by the terrifying lack of sensitivity in Charlotte's daughter, Luciane, on the occasion of her visit to a sick girl who had caused the death of a little sister. By forcing the unfortunate girl to appear in public, she causes her to lose her mental balance forever. If the contrast between Luciane and Ottilie had always been emphasized, it achieves, on that occasion, its crowning irony.

The insensitive minor characters are thus ironically placed in the midst of the hypersensitive main figures who realize each other's emotions and wishes almost before they enter the person's own consciousness.

But there are sensitive characters around them, too. The two men in love with Ottilie, the apprentice-teacher and the young architect, mirror in many ways Ottilie's own sensitive relationship to her environment. Just as she involuntarily imitates Eduard's handwriting, the architect, equally unconsciously, paints her likeness in the angel faces in the chapel. The architect's and Ottilie's loves have an unconscious innocence which would seem to protect them from tragedy.

In talking about Mittler, I used the term "ironic symbol." The mode most characteristic of the style of *Elective Affinities* is precisely its ironic symbolism. In trying to define this term, however, we run into difficulties; for not all the symbolism of the work is ironic and, conversely, not all irony symbolic. I will, therefore, discuss the symbolic structure and the ironic stance separately, bringing the two together in the end.

The title and the chemical image are, of course, the first symbols which the reader discovers. He does not realize, however, that both the moss-hut in which the chemical image is discussed, and the path leading to it are symbols typical of Charlotte's careful and orderly, but not very farsighted, planning. As the story unfolds, the moss-hut will be forgotten and Ottilie's "Lusthaus" will take its place. The moss-hut was small and built just for two persons, whereas the "Lusthaus" with its wide view, from which the castle cannot be seen, is big enough to house the women and the baby. It looks down on the ponds in which the child will drown, and while he is drowning, Ottilie can see the last rays of the evening sun reflected in its windows. With the sinking of the sun, Ottilie's hope fades forever.

This is one example out of many which show Goethe's extremely careful use of symbolism. There is no tree, no flower and no water which does not symbolize the main events. The same is true of the secondary characters, including, of course, the child itself. While, to all appearances, proceeding in a realistic manner by placing events in a concrete context, Goethe uses this carefully described environment to point symbolically at the meaning of the work. But these realistic descriptions become symbolic only if the author consciously places them in an over-all symbolic treatment. The moss-hut, used by itself, may become typical of Charlotte's character, but in the context of the entire novel it becomes symbolic only by its contrast to the "Lusthaus." At this point, we realize that it is not only a symbol, but in fact a highly ironic one because it symbolizes the togetherness of Charlotte and her husband, which comes to an end at the very beginning of the novel when the Captain appears. The elective affinities are, ironically, discussed in the moss-hut. The path leading upward from it is not even finished when the whole plan collapses.

The entire work has to be read in this fashion. Such a reading will result in the realization that the novel as a whole has a symbolic structure, consisting of symbols which mirror present events and foreshadow future ones at a time when the characters cannot possibly understand their meaning. The reader, however, if he is sensitive to Goethe's procedure, should realize that a clue has been given to him which tells him to be on guard. If we know the author at all, the moss-hut cannot be the pastime of Charlotte's idle days. It is a signal given by the author to the reader. How ironic it is we will learn much later.

Irony in the *Elective Affinities* thus seems to be the discrepancy between what the omniscient narrator knows and what the characters cannot possibly know. It is hinted at in discreet ways, and only a very careful reading reveals its constant presence. The distant, omniscient narrator casts his objective glance at the events and, knowing the entire truth, cannot but warn or pity his misled characters. Not being able to change the course of events, which is ineluctable, he can only indicate to the reader that he ought to be more watchful than the characters, who are caught up in their own destiny.

Not all of this irony is expressed in foreshadowing symbols. Some of it inheres imperceptibly in the narrative. Like ancient tragic irony, this is the irony of the events themselves. Thus, after both Eduard and Charlotte had lost their mates, Charlotte introduces Eduard to Ottilie in the hope, understood only much later, that he might marry her.

The chemical affinities, too, are misinterpreted by Eduard, who is, to be sure, blinder than any of the other participants. He asks Charlotte to invite Ottilie because he fears that she will be lonely while he is working with (in chemical terms: attracted to) the Captain. The irony of this misinterpretation is made apparent only a few pages later when the activities of the four people require their regrouping in an appanently very natural and rational way: Charlotte will have to work with the Captain on changes in her plans concerning the moss-hut. Ottilie is thus forced into the company of Eduard.

Thus irony as the true stance of the author is all-pervasive. Only the narrator's favorite figure Ottilie is entirely exempt from it. This is in part explained by Ottilie's close relationship to nature. Irony cannot be applied to nature, nor to a character unconsciously and unknowingly obeying natural laws, while it is easily applicable to characters with a "sentimental" relationship to nature. Ottilie, however, is an utterly unsentimental character.[14]

Much of the novel takes place outdoors, and not by accident. The castle itself is never described, in fact its architectural plan remains vague. By contrast, the outdoor world is clearly delineated. Goethe distinguishes between the garden, symbol of Eduard's past activities, and the free and open landscape to which the ponds belong. Eduard and Ottilie spend their happiest moments near these ponds which, after being united into one lake, bring nothing but unhappiness. Ottilie is happiest outdoors, more than anyone else a child of nature, growing herself, like trees or flowers, unconsciously from adolescence into adulthood. She is attracted to water, and her recurring headaches arise from subterranean waters. She is thus an elemental force whose relationship to Eduard, characterized by an unconscious attraction, turns out to be like a catastrophe, carrying with it, in its ineluctable course, all the persons involved, their plans, their conventions, and even their convictions. True love, Goethe seems to say, is a natural event, and nature, as he often emphasized, is indifferent to moral good and evil.

But Ottilie, who, as has been seen above, is quite unconscious for most of the novel of the disaster she has caused, awakens after the death of the child to her true condition. While she cannot stop loving Eduard, she can renounce him, and this she does relentlessly. After they are all reunited at the castle, they seem, ironically, to take up the life they had led a year earlier before it was so tragically interrupted. Only Ottilie has changed. She is now the only knowing one, the only person who fully understands the whole situation. The others are still trying to mend it, at least partially. Destiny, which had led her blindly into disaster, has opened her eyes, and she knows that she must die. But she does not speak, and only in her last letter to her friends does she express the truth her conscience has taught her: "I have strayed from my course, and I shall not find it again." In contrast to the chemical elements, a human being has one choice left after the natural affinities have done their ruinous work: Goethe's word for this human effort is resignation, a state of mind he simultaneously fights and accepts. In *Elective Affinities*, it leads to the death of Ottilie and, in imitation of her, of Eduard. They will be buried together in the chapel which bears the mark of the architect's love of Ottilie in the angel faces on the ceiling. And the grave will be for Charlotte the definite locus of their memory—in ironic contrast to her initial effort to remove graves from their original site. The miracle that Ottilie's body seems to perform in the end is not meant to be a true miracle—it is rather a symbol of Ottilie's overcoming of her earthly wishes to be Eduard's, when it has become clear that she will be his for eternity. Her earthly resignation transforms her love into something everlasting.

In terms of "polarity" and "Steigerung," the return of the

human mind to the World Spirit can, as in *Faust*, take place only after death. But this is not a Christian resurrection; it is rather the gradual overcoming of the body in favor of a purer spirituality. Although on a realistic level, Ottilie commits suicide by starvation, this thought does not strike the reader's mind. We understand that a different kind of purification takes place, far removed from moral atonement or from suicide as evasion. Ottilie, the child of nature, surpasses nature in an apotheosis similar to that of *Faust*. The suffering and, in moral terms, guilty person regains her innocence when she leaves her body behind. No remission of sins is needed—her death, like everybody's death, *is* her purification.

CHAPTER 6

Goethe and the French Revolution

I Introductory Remarks

BEFORE we continue our discussion of the genres which Goethe employed, we have to insert a historical consideration much needed for the genre of the tale. Goethe generally avoided interjecting specific contemporary events into his work. He preferred to bypass the trivialities of the day in favor of more general and universally valid expressions of the human mind. However, the French Revolution can hardly be called trivial, and Goethe fully realized its enormity. Like most of his German contemporaries, he reacted with horror to the bloody deeds of the men of the *Terreur.* He saw the persecutions and the death of the innocent and guilty alike, and his heart was on the side of the persecuted. The young Goethe had been a rebel, but not a revolutionary. Of politics he knew little except the court intrigues at Weimar. With the sense of humaneness he had acquired in Italy, he could hardly be expected to take the side of Danton or Robespierre.

Even Schiller, a more violent rebel in his youth and a man with a vast knowledge of history and the political workings of the kings and leaders, could not greet the bloody revolution with joy, and most Germans to whom the impoverished refugees came for help felt exactly the same way.[1] The American Revolution had excited their minds and filled them with great hopes for an improvement in social conditions and a guarantee of human freedom. The French Revolution seemed to contradict all ideas of the Enlightenment. There was no improvement, but only Terror and a new kind of tyranny.

II The Comedies of the Revolution

It seems strange, nevertheless, to see that Goethe's first reaction to the historic event was an attempt to ridicule its followers by writing comedies about them. What he ridiculed—and it must be said that the two comedies (*Der Bürgergeneral* and *Die Aufgeregten* [The Excited Ones]) are not very successful—was the Third Estate in Germany, which tried to imitate the successful French Tiers-Etat.

According to Aristotelian comedy, only the lower classes should be ridiculed in Comedy—this is precisely what Goethe tries to do. The plays, according to rule, are written in prose, and the comic stance of the "leaders" of a ridiculous rebellion is made clear from the start. But the first play is short and the second incomplete. Somehow comedy does not work when the issues are serious, and Goethe was well aware of the utter seriousness of the social issues. While it is true that he could not quite conceive of a society in which the Estates of aristocracy, bourgeoisie and lower class would be completely abolished and eliminated, he felt that the burden of honesty and fairness was squarely on the upper classes who must prove themselves worthy of their wealth and their position. In the third act of *The Excited Ones*, the Countess, against whose estate some of the rebellion is directed, speaks some passionately felt lines on the subject of the Estates:

Ever since I saw with my own eyes that human nature may be pushed and humiliated to an incredible degree, but cannot be suppressed and annihilated, I decided that every action which seems unfair to me must be strictly avoided by myself, and that I must clearly express my opinion on such actions in my family, in society, at Court. I will not remain silent in the face of injustice. I will not tolerate smallness of mind which hides under big pomp—even if I should be known by the hateful name of a democrat.

Unfortunately, the rest of this act is unfinished; but we know that the Countess will eventually pour out her feelings. It is equally clear that the daughter of the Countess is very immature, taking hard-headedly the side of her Estate and insisting on her "rights" to her property. Goethe marks this as a decided flaw. This evaluation of the daughter becomes important in the context of the only tragedy Goethe wrote on the Revolution.

III The Natural Daughter

The play, one part of a planned trilogy, was written only a few years after *The Excited Ones*. This trilogy, of whose unfinished parts we have only a few hints and short titles, was to express Goethe's overall views of politics in general and the fatal period of the French Revolution in particular. By the time he was working on it (1799–1803), however, the Revolution had been defeated by Napoleon and the pressing social problems had lost their immediate appeal.

Goethe's mind operated fruitfully only when he could raise practical problems onto a high level of general validity. Thus, in *The Natural Daughter*, he deprived the immediate (largely practical) problems created by the Revolution of their urgency and concreteness. And while the play hints at intrigues and a general restlessness, the characteristic features of the Revolution of 1789 give way to some rather mysterious allusions, to dissatisfaction with the king and similar "general" political phenomena which might occur at any time in history. The natural daughter, child of a duke, is the blind victim of such generalized political events, and any flavor relating to a specific country is entirely lost. We are not prepared to state that this is a bad play, but it certainly lacks historical color. Raised by her father to be a proud aristocratic woman, Eugenie finds it hard to be saved from a life of exile in the French colonies by a very decent bourgeois who is willing to marry her. In contrast to Natalie in *Wilhelm Meister*, which had been finished only three years earlier, this young noblewoman has a vastly exaggerated, entirely undemocratic view of the aristocracy. No doubt, as a writer, Goethe always acted like an actor who with each different role dons a different mask. To state that he was undemocratic is as wrong as to maintain that he was a dedicated democrat. He presented each problem at its time and place and in its particular environment. Natalie's enlightened environment made it unproblematic for her to marry the bourgeois Wilhelm, whereas Eugenie's hardheaded aristocratic environment had endowed her with a strong sense of her place in the hierarchical order. In her case, this stance is enhanced by the fact of her illegitimate birth. She is removed from the court at the very moment when she hoped to be fully accepted by the King as her father's child and the king's relative. From her peculiar vantage point, it is plausible that she reacts against a bourgeois marriage, just as it is plausible for Natalie not even to ask about Wilhelm's origin. Goethe treats his characters aesthetically—no other consideration could alter this prime demand he made on his productions. His purpose was never to convey political messages, but rather to present each subject matter on its own merits. And we, who are used to finding messages in plays, would be treated rather harshly by an author who finds the creation of plays with "messages" beneath his dignity as a writer.

IV   Hermann und Dorothea

Goethe produced only one really great work on the effects of the French Revolution: the idyl *Hermann und Dorothea*, which was written shortly after the French had raided Weimar (1796–97), while Goethe was fully aware both of the hardships of war and the blessings of peace. At that time, his love of antiquity was still great and it is natural that he wrote this most German of his works in hexameters. *Hermann und Dorothea* also offers many reminders of Homer, even more so than the early parts of *Werther*, which are also filled with Homeric allusions. Goethe still considered Homer an idyllic rather than an heroic author, thinking of such parts of the *Odyssey* as Odysseus' meeting with Nausicaa —a theme he intended to treat in dramatic form. *Hermann und Dorothea* consists of nine parts, each labeled after one of the Muses. However, even in doing this, he changed the work from an ancient into a modern work. Under the name of each Muse, Goethe added a subtitle, which indicates the actual, although somewhat generalized course of the action. These subtitles show what Goethe was really aiming at. They are: Fate and Sympathy, Hermann, The Citizens (with the connotation "bourgeois"), Mother and Son, the Citizen of the World, the Contemporary Scene, Dorothea (which means the Goddess of Gifts), Hermann and Dorothea, and View into the Future. In Part Five, it is not immediately clear who the "Citizen of the World" is; it might be Hermann or the Pastor of his town who accompanies him, or the "Judge" who is the leader of the refugees. All three have an unprejudiced view of man; they do not care about possessions or a career, but rather look at the true worth of a person. Goethe uses the refugees and their problems as specific examples of an often repeated occurrence in history—a tendency indicated by the subtitles—and he lets the Pastor address the Judge in the following manner:

Yes, you appear today like one of the oldest leaders, who guided the
exiled peoples through deserts and wastes, I almost think I am talking
to Joshua or Moses.

To which the Judge, now clearly considered to be the citizen
of the world replies:

Indeed, our era resembles the oddest eras History records, sacred
as well as profane.

The biblical as well as the Homeric background, point to the
wider view which Goethe always aspired to: a present tragedy
is always the reflection of similar, past or future tragedies—inevitable and terrible, but understandable only as a universal
condition of man.

It is Goethe himself, the Citizen of the World, who observed
the Revolution and understood its almost inevitable consequences.
In the part on the Contemporary Scene, the Judge speaks about
the Revolution. Who can deny, he says, that everyone's heart
was moved when men first heard of the "right of man that is
common to all, of freedom and cherished equality." Even
when the first revolutionary armies came to their land, everybody
hoped that the highest condition man can think of might be
near and within reach. But only too soon selfishness and the drive
for power destroyed the idealistic stance of the first revolutionary
generation. War started, and with it the bitterness and brutality
typical of a defeated army. The town from which the refugees
came [2] was drawn into the conflict between the revolutionary
and anti-revolutionary forces, compelling the civilians to flee with
whatever they could save.

This is a fair and wise evaluation. In the context of this particular work, the ultimate meaning of the Revolution is to remind
the reader—and, above all, the wealthy townspeople—of the frailty
of human fortune and the utter need for unselfish sympathy in
times of despair. Hermann's mother had fostered this trait in her
son, whom she sends to the refugees with food and old clothes.
And he meets the refugee girl, Dorothea, being herself a symbol
of unselfish devotion, at the moment when she needs old clothing
for a mother and her new-born baby. The father, on the other
hand, having himself created the family fortune through hard

work, would prefer a wealthy daughter-in-law. Fortunately, his friends, the Pastor and the apothecary, help, with ample wisdom and a great sense of humor, to set the old man right. And whereas Goethe cannot but treat the well-to-do bourgeois with a great deal of irony, he simultaneously wanted to make the readers like him. With delightful humor, he strikes a perfect balance between the double perspective he wants us to apply to the innkeeper of the Golden Lion, i.e., irony and sympathy.

The little work is a perfect jewel, not only with regard to its gentle irony and kind humor, but also from the point of view of a perfectly integrated form. I can't begin here to enumerate its many subtle implications, which round out the simple plot and make it a meaningful and impressive whole—as e.g. the fact that Hermann's parents, too, had married after a great misfortune (a fire that destroyed much of the town), and many others. However I would like to point at the careful realism which Goethe used—more than in any other of his works—to give his story the small-town, and yet still agricultural, background needed as contrast to the homelessness of the refugees. Thus he portrays Hermann's mother walking through their property in search of her son—and takes pains to make this property sound rich and firmly grounded in solid labor.[3] A pear-tree at the end of the property marks the boundary, and it is under that tree that, somewhat later, Hermann and Dorothea sit down under the full moon to overlook what will be her future home. The idyl, thus, seems complete. And yet, the author himself would have felt hemmed in by such a perfect agrarian situation. At this time of his life, only the smallest industrial efforts had been made, and Goethe was greatly interested in them. The agrarian idyl of *Hermann und Dorothea* is not meant as a contrast to industrial society, but as a contrast to the homeless refugees. Goethe was too fully aware of the precariousness of ownership to set it up as an ideal life. But in this one short work it is a good thing, and although the bourgeois father is gently mocked, being also a wealthy townsman who owns his land, he seems in a good position to help the poor. Never again will we find in Goethe's work the rising middle-class depicted as a haven. But here it has, in Goethe's estimation, a perfect place.

No doubt, in the decade after the Revolution, Goethe was more interested in sociological questions than at any other time. *Wil-*

helm Meister is a perfect example of this preoccupation. The Revolution did not transform the poet, who was in his forties, into a "radical," but it did make him aware of the social problems he had largely ignored as a subject matter of his writing. After *The Natural Daughter* he no longer treated social problems thematically. But for the ten or twelve years following the French Revolution he tried to incorporate these issues—which were never very close to his heart—in various ways into his work.

CHAPTER 7

Tales

I   *Introductory Remarks*

THE term "Erzählung," equivalent to the French "conte," was used by Goethe in preference to the Italian term "novella." In his mature years, it became one of his favorite genres. The French term had been broadly applied to a number of literary forms: "philosophic tales" (often satiric ones, such as Voltaire's *Candide*) or dialogues, such as Voltaire's *Micromégas*. Or it could be a sentimental tale, such as Diderot's *Les Deux Amis de Bourbonne*. It was told in either the first or the third person. It could be a longer narrative or center around a single event. One of its main characteristics, inherent in its name, is the fact that it is *told* by someone, usually orally, to an audience. Goethe was well aware of this tradition and used it frequently. Since the tale was essentially a product of the late Middle Ages, during which much of its complexities had developed, and since it had been used only in late antiquity, long after Aristotle had "frozen" the dramatic genres, it offered a great deal of individual freedom. No rules were set down for it by anybody who had used it; it had an evasive quality that was appealing to someone with Goethe's interest in new forms.

As an acceptable literary genre, the "Erzählung" was introduced into German literature by Goethe himself. He also introduced the term *Novelle*, which became the favorite term and type of narrative throughout nineteenth-century German literature. Goethe sought to make distinctions between these various types of shorter stories, calling them "Erzählung," "Märchen," "Novelle," according to certain distinctive marks and characteristics. But these distinctions can be discussed only in the particular context of the various tales, since he did not establish any basic code.

In many ways, Goethe preferred the old, well-known and well-tried presentation of a series of tales within a single larger narrative framework. He did this in two ways. The first—which occurs in his first attempt at tale-writing—resembles Boccaccio's *Decameron,* inasmuch as the tales are told orally by a group of storytellers and are strung together like beads in a necklace. One follows the other, and while the framework has its own value and dignity, it would barely carry any weight without the string of individual stories. By and large, this is the method of the *Unterhaltungen deutscher Ausgewanderten* (*Conversations of German Refugees*).

The second method is that of inserting the tale into a work of larger proportion, which could exist without it but is enriched and rendered more significant by it. Such are the inserted tales in *Fiction and Truth* and in *Elective Affinities. Wilhelm Meister's Years of Wandering* can almost be considered a fusion of the two methods. The only tale which does not form part of a larger work is that which is simply called *Novelle.*

Goethe always keeps up the fiction that a tale is a form of direct communication, either told to an audience or written down by the person whom the event concerns or by someone near that person. He enjoyed writing such tales since they retained, in his judgment, the lightness of the older, truly oral examples of the species. Except for the *Novelle,* he did not treat them with the seriousness with which he approached his novels or plays. Goethe was obviously self-conscious when he set out to tell tales. Critical remarks are interspersed either between stories or in the stories themselves, as for example in "Der Mann von fünfzig Jahren" (The Man of Fifty Years), which forms part of the *Wanderjahre.*

Aside from the formal tales in the novels, i.e., those that are set off by a title, such as the "Die wunderlichen Nachbarkinder" (Amazing Young Neighbors) in *Elective Affinities* or the "Der junge Paris" (Young Paris) in *Fiction and Truth,* the novels contain a number of stories told by or about individual characters concerning their past, with all the earmarks of a "tale." Both the formal and the "informal" tales are connected with the novels not only because they contain events that happened to one of the characters, but through various themes they have in common with the principal themes of the novels, and the effect they exercise upon the principal characters. Such informal tales are, in *Elective Affinities*, the story of the visiting Englishman, and, in *Wilhelm Meister*, the reports on the past of Mignon and the harpist. The entire sixth book of *Wilhelm Meister*, "Bekenntnisse einer schönen Seele" (Confessions of a Beautiful Soul) is nothing but a tale (with its own title), which is inserted because both thematically and by its characters, it is closely related to the main plot of the novel.

It seems that Goethe was strongly attracted by the mere pleasure of telling a story that reports an "extraordinary event." The great joy of storytelling, so prevalent in the Middle-Ages and throughout the Renaissance and almost unknown in our own world, had considerable appeal to an author who claimed to have inherited from his mother the "joy of telling stories" (*die Lust am Fabulieren*). Not all of these tales are of Goethe's own invention. The poet drew as freely as earlier storytellers on a wealth of familiar stories translating them into German. This method belongs to the older genre, which was still partly based on oral tradition. Had Goethe lived earlier, and had he not written poems as well as prose in a much more modern vein, he might be counted among the great storytellers, such as Boccaccio, Chaucer, the collector of the *Cent nouvelles nouvelles*, etc.

Goethe came too late for that genre, and was ready only in a limited way for the more modern short story. From a modern viewpoint many of his tales, particularly the earlier ones, suffer from several defects. In the first place, they are told for the sake of an interesting, mostly odd or strange, "event." The characterization of persons is not the chief object of the author's endeavor. The characters get themselves into "unnatural" situations, and the reader awaits, with greater or lesser suspense, the solution of the dilemma. Although it does not necessarily follow from this premise, in many of Goethe's tales the emphasis is much more on plot than on character. Most of the characters in these tales are insipid stereotypes. There are young girls, beautiful widows, a major, a son, etc., who play their particular part in the development of events, on which they may or may not have any influence. They become involved in events which are only marginally shaped by their own characteristic behavior. Somehow, with more or less grace or wisdom, they live through these events. They don't behave in any extraordinary way; a few of them try to do "the right thing," as they see it in the light of their present, incom-

plete understanding. However, not only the characters are unim-
portant, but, in contrast to Goethe's practice in his major novels,
the setting is even more so. There is little symbolism; the "castle,"
or the "nice little house" is the only setting, and Goethe makes
no attempt at that careful elaboration which is so typical of his
larger prose-works.

However, although also suffering from the defects just mentioned, most of the tales inserted in the *Wanderjahre* present
strong and credible emotions and are at times quite moving. In
contrast to his earlier tales, they actually touch the reader's heart.
On the other hand, they are as little philosophical as these earlier
ones. They may be marginally "moral," something which the Baroness in the *Unterhaltungen* particularly likes, and which gives
rise to conversations on morality. But, on the whole, even the
moral interest is subordinated to the presentation of the central
event. That the tales in the *Wanderjahre* serve a more important
function within the frame of the novel is, of course, true. But
since most of them can be removed from their context, a discussion of their formal aspects seems entirely justified.

II Unterhaltungen der deutscher Ausgewanderten

Written in 1797, this somewhat fragmentary work has, as was
said before, a framework most clearly reminiscent of the *Decameron*. A group of German aristocrats, having had to flee from the
French revolutionary troops invading Germany, finds itself
stranded at one of the Baroness' estates. After some refugee
friends arrive, a political quarrel breaks out, which causes the
friends to leave in a huff and forces the Baroness to require a
more civil behavior in the future by avoiding political discussions
in polite society. It is against this background of both immediate
need and the urge to escape from it that an old minister tells
the first tale.

In accord with the general looseness of the frame, a dialogue
is inserted after the departure of the friends and before the beginning of the old man's tale. Toward the end of this dialogue,
Goethe comes as close as he ever did to formulating a theory of
the "tale." Tales must be entertaining and sufficiently "new,"
he says, in order to hold the interest of a group that has so many
real worries and troubles and harbors so many disturbing, serious
opinions. Over the years, the old man has collected such stories

which give "an unexpected insight into human nature and its hidden motivations." Other stories reveal oddities of behavior which amuse him. In one way or another they all have touched his mind or heart and produced in him a "moment of calm serenity." He is not interested in scandals but, rather, in the emotions which bring together or separate men and women. He likes stories in which man finds himself at odds with his own self, his desires and intentions; or in which mere chance plays with human weakness and imperfection. And he is anxious that his heroes should be neither blamed nor praised. He makes his listeners particularly curious with the remark that anything "miraculous" arouses the interest of the audience.

The points related so far pertain to a theory of content rather than form—and its liberality permits almost any topic to be treated in the genre. One criterion seems to be stable, however, namely that of entertaining an audience by a story told orally. The social (one might almost say, aristocratic) function of the tale is emphasized, and so, in contrast to Voltaire's tales, is the absence of political content. The author makes it very clear that, while the storytellers are political refugees and one of them strongly sympathizes with the revolt of the masses, storytelling is a refined and unpolitical occupation. Therefore, the old minister stresses the universal quality of these stories which might take place at any historical time because they deal exclusively with universal human relationships. The audience of these tales is not restricted to a listening role, but may, at any moment, become active and contribute additional tales or criticize the ones just heard.

When he wrote the *Unterhaltungen*, Goethe experimented with different types of tales. The first two deal with "poltergeists," the last two before the *Märchen* are called "moral" tales, and the last one is the "Fairytale" which, from the point of view of aesthetic quality, is infinitely superior to the rest and will therefore be discussed here. The others do not require a detailed analysis.

III Märchen

After two "moral tales" have been told by the old man of the *Unterhaltungen*, he promises a tale that is entirely a product of the imagination and which, as he puts it, "should remind us of nothing and everything." One of the participants in the preceding conversations had suggested that purely imaginative works such as fairy tales should carefully avoid giving the appearance of realism or rationality, but should instead "play on us like music and move us within ourselves to the extent that we forget that something outside of us produces this movement." The notion of this movement within us which is produced by purely imaginary works is closely akin to what Schiller called *Spiel* and what he considered to be the main function not only of fairy tales but of *all* works of art. It is in this spirit, then, that Goethe's *Märchen* must be read, and we must be careful to refrain from over-interpretating and, above all, over-rationalizing it. If not everything in the *Märchen* can be explained, this is entirely in keeping with Goethe's purpose. What we don't understand will, nonetheless, be pleasing to our imagination, which is, and should be, willing to go along with the premises of the story regardless of their rational or realistic basis. The light motion of the mind caused by the movement of the author's imagination is not jarred by any violent interruption. The author sets the pace, and creates and moves the "characters," the "incidents," even the meaning according to the rules of his imagination which he restrains against excess violence or abrupt change. Once he has established his set of rules he abides by them, much as a composer does once he has chosen his themes, key, and over-all format. This well bridled imagination produces the perfect work of art which Schiller asked for.

The "art fairy tale" (Kunstmärchen) seems to be a peculiarly German art-form. It is not based on folk fairy tales and has entirely different characters and plots. It borrows from the simpler folk-tales the elements of unrealistic or miraculous events, of number and color symbolism, of a strict design and a perfect solution. We may be confronted with cruelty and apparent death, but there will needs be a happy ending. Guilt and punishment will be carefully weighed and clearly established, and good and evil would seem to be clearer than they can ever be in any more "realistic" art-form. Some of the Romantic authors, above all Novalis and, somewhat later, E.T.A. Hoffmann used this form to great advantage, and it was taken up by as modern an author as Hugo von Hofmannsthal. Its appeal is still the one Goethe described in the few paragraphs which precede the *Märchen* of the *Unterhaltungen*.

It must be added that the authors just mentioned were particularly well acquainted with the much older alchemical fairy tales, which were tales symbolical of the process of making gold. But since for many of these authors the making of gold had a spiritual value, being the symbolic presentation of the salvation of the soul and the vision of God, the steps for the production of gold are, simultaneously, steps on the way to salvation. These tales were highly symbolic, rich in number and color symbolism, strange and fascinating in their use of symbols, and their material was highly adaptable to a more modern and conscious art-form. All authors mentioned above, including Goethe, drew heavily on this older material.

Oddly enough, the *Unterhaltungen* are never resumed after the *Märchen*. Obviously, the latter satisfied Goethe to the extent that he felt no need to complete the cycle—if it was ever seriously considered as a major project. If Goethe's main object in the *Unterhaltungen* was to offer some loose thoughts on the topic of "Tales," the *Märchen* was to him the most satisfying example, surpassing in its quality all the preceding tales. It presents the real goal of Goethe's ambitions, a perfect "poetic" art-work which left nothing to be desired.

Its poetic premises can be grasped easily. A river separates two vastly different realms which might roughly be equated to those of death and of life. In the course of the tale, the river is crossed by various characters in both directions by different means of transportation: the Ferryman transports passengers only from the Eastern to the Western bank, while a giant's shadow returns the guests to the Eastern bank. The mainstream of visitors is carried by the Ferryman toward the realm of the Lily which is, in some ways, the realm of death. In the end, however, she and everyone else cross the bridge, built through the self-sacrifice of the Serpent, and returns to the realm from where all the characters had come to her and which I will call, for the sake of clarity, the realm of the Temple, i.e., that of life. It is equally clear that the realm of the Lily is on the Western, i.e., the death-producing, bank of the river because the Giant who stands there throws his shadow across the river in the evening sun. On the other hand, when, in the end, they are all united on the Eastern bank, the light of the morning-sun is reflected on them by the magic mirror held in the claws of the Hawk.

[158]

The great opposites in this magic world are not only day and night or light and darkness, but, above all, life and death, or perhaps better living things and dead things. Thus it is characteristic that the wife of the Man-with-the-Lamp can carry dead weights on her head with ease, but is weighed down by such lightweight living things as the vegetables she is bringing to the river. Another pair of opposites is constituted by the vegetable and mineral realms. The river refuses to accept gold, and its Ferryman must be paid in vegetables.

The Lily who lives on the Western Bank kills the life she touches, but apparently restores life to a dog who had been turned into stone. In her realm, she can grow trees, but no plant bearing flowers or fruit can grow there. She is beautiful and can sing, but she has been kept from love and life.

The Man-with-the-Lamp, who belongs to the Temple side of the river and who, as the lamp indicates, knows what others do not know, is her guardian and protector. He knows about the power of life and death, but he also knows about that of gold, silver and iron, the symbols of force. He does not precipitate the events but understands their meaning. His lamp is healing and life-preserving during the "decisive night," and he has faith in the future. He also knows that great goals can be achieved only when many work together in "the propitious hour." That the Lily has to be freed from her garden of infertility is clear to her as it is to everyone else, and it is obvious that only love will do this. It is when the Prince is willing to die in her arms rather than live without her that things begin to happen. While he lies lifeless, precariously protected by the magic circle of the Serpent, the final events before the breakthrough into life are being prepared. Just as the Prince preferred death to sterile life, the wise Serpent realizes that the sacrifice of her life is needed in order to revive him. And in this amazing exchange of life for death, and death for life, not only are the Prince and the Lily blessed with the life of love and happiness, but their realm is suddenly crowded with their future subjects, who cross the new bridge easily in both directions. There is no more separation between the banks. Thanks to the presents of the three underground Kings, the Prince turns from a love-sick boy into an active man, and the Lily's long period of sterility is ended.

It is easy enough to read many of Goethe's favorite thoughts into this fairy tale. It is a classical work in which each character has his particular task to contribute to the welfare of all, reminding us of the Society of the Tower in *Wilhelm Meister*. The Temple actually is described as classical in its design. The gentle light of the lamp is the light of the sages, of which we find examples in *Wilhelm Meisters Wanderjahre*.

On another level, this is a nature myth, showing the great faith which Goethe had in the power of life and its constant renewal. The poem *Selige Sehnsucht* was written with a similar faith in the regenerative powers of life. On still another level, this is the eternal fairy tale that takes place between man and woman, i.e., the awakening of both through the power of love. There is also the sense of constant movement, of transformation and change, so dear to Goethe's thought.

With all of this clearly implied, the real joy in reading the *Märchen* does not consist in turning it into allegory by trying to find its exact meaning. It is, after all, in Goethe's sense a tale and carries all the delight a perfect tale may create. There are mysterious happenings which find unexpected solutions; there is a great deal of humor and an over-all lightness of touch which is deftly handled to make the reader simultaneously attentive, curious, sympathetic, melancholy, and smiling. Some light eighteenth-century music might accompany the whole, with its sad and sprightly passages, its over-all elegance and its charm. I would hate to see something as perfectly worked out as this little jewel turned into a weighty message about life and death. Grief and death are there—but only in a fairy-tale way.

IV *Novelle*

Written in 1827, this little narrative has a charm and distinction all its own. Not being designed as part of a collection of tales it had, according to Goethe's aesthetic judgment, to carry its own weight in order to come up to his standards of perfection. At this late stage in his life Goethe's ever-growing tendency was to write, both in poetry and in prose, only such works as contain some symbolic, or even allegorical, meaning. These works are not easy to decipher. Goethe kept them, on their literal level, in a state of poetic suspense and tension. They are "beautiful," i.e., things of beauty to be looked at and admired regardless of possible meanings. And a certain delight in a deliberate mystification of the reader is not foreign to the aging author. In the *Novelle*, we are faced with a small, but highly perfected work of art, a work, moreover, that has no parallel in either contemporary works or his own output.

The story's content is quickly told. The young wife of a Prince (*Fürst*) watches her husband and his followers leave for a hunt. As she stands at the window, following with her eyes the train of hunters, she sees, on the other side of the valley, the ruins of the old family castle which is about to be restored. An uncle shows her the architectural plans for the restoration, and they decide to visit the castle, accompanied by the young page Honorio (the only character with a name). On its way to the ruins, the group has to pass through a little town where a group of "artists" is holding a fair. In one tent, a tiger and a lion are kept safely for future performances. Above the tent there is a picture of these animals with grim expressions, which reminds the uncle of a fire he had once seen break out on the occasion of a similar fair.

As the group, standing in the old castle around noontime, look back at the town, a quickly spreading fire actually does break out there. The wild animals are set free by the fire, and the tiger pursues the Princess who, having moved toward the town, gallops back toward the old ruins they had left when they discovered the fire. Honorio, who is vaguely in love with the young Princess, kills the tiger. At that moment, the owners of the animals, a gypsy couple and their young son, appear, desperate about the death of their tiger. In the meantime, the lion appears and stalks into the old castle ruins. The Prince, having returned from the hunt with his followers, is asked by the gypsies to spare the lion, whom the little boy can surely tame. The permission is granted, and the boy plays the flute accompanying his father's religious hymn. The music tames the wild beast who obediently follows his young master.

I would like to interpret this mysterious work from the point of view of the interaction between nature and culture or, to put it somewhat differently, between the raw forces of nature and the cultivating ones of man. I am sure that this is not the only viewpoint from which the tale can be understood, but I find that it can be applied with great consistency and is, as far as I can see, the only completely satisfactory one, inasmuch as every detail of the story can be encompassed by it.

Neither are the forces of nature, as presented in the tale, all "raw," nor is man's cultivating power over nature totally "good." The story is much too complex to allow for easy generalizations; and only the final answer to the perplexing problem of the relationship between man and nature, namely the overwhelming power of love in man, seems to offer anything in the way of a "solution." But it would be too simple to accept even this final answer as the tale's "moral." Goethe was much too aware of the instability of human existence to offer this solution in any form other than that of a fairy tale.

The tale opens at one of Goethe's well-known "castles," [1] whose very site makes it interesting and, with regard to the entire tale, meaningful. It is situated on a hillside, thus overlooking not only a long river valley and the mountains beyond the river, but also the ruins of the original family castle, located on the opposite hillside. The town at the foot of the hill, through which the owners of the castle ride to visit the old castle, is obviously not visible from the modern one, but very clearly within sight of the ruins.

Although much interested in modern economic problems, the young Prince sets them aside and sets out instead for a big hunt to "stir up (*beunruhigen*) the peaceful inhabitants of the distant forests by an unexpected campaign" (*Kriegszug*). We cannot immediately understand the symbolic allusion of this sentence which occurs on the second page of the tale. But considering the taming of the lion by the young boy at the end of the story the author's irony is obvious. Man, and not the lion, turns out to be the killer. It is a first ironic reference to the theme of "man versus nature."

After having watched the hunters depart, the young countess turns her attention to the old castle, and the princely uncle enters with plans for its restoration. In the rest of the story, the new castle is forgotten and the old becomes the center of events. The reason for this change of locale and emphasis may simply be the fact that the fairy-tale ending is more in agreement with the old setting; but one can go one step further. The new castle is seen from man's perspective, and the old one from that of nature. With his modern economic interests, his attempts to benefit his subjects and himself simultaneously, the count lives indeed in the world of man, and his thinking is positive and practical.

In the old castle, on the other hand, nature has taken over from man. The trees have plunged their roots into the cracks, and the whole place shows "how the old traces of human power, which has long since disappeared, are seen in the great struggle with the eternally living and generating force of nature." There are also granite rocks "untouched by any change," no matter whether produced by man or nature. The conflicts depicted in the tale are most fittingly set in this locale of elemental conflicts.

From beginning to end, the plot is loaded with ironic contrasts. The gay hunt, lovingly described at the beginning, is prematurely interrupted because of the fire that breaks out at the fair. Instead of the deer, the tiger is killed by the young Honorio. Oddly enough this is an unnecessary and harmful action because, without Honorio chasing the tiger, the latter would not have run after the Princess. During their ride through the town, they had just seen the picture of that same tiger, and the uncle had commented on this picture above the entrance to the tiger-booth. In the picture, the animal is wildly attacking a Moor, whereas the real tiger lies peacefully in his cage. It was only man's imagination, not reality, which had created the picture.

The hunt which is not carried out is similar to the visit to the old castle. Whether or not the castle will be rebuilt, we do not know. The visit, at any rate, is rudely interrupted by the elemental forces which threaten the very lives of the visitors.

Another irony exists in the uncle's uneasiness concerning the ride through the fair, since it reminds him of the fire he had witnessed earlier. No fire breaks out during the visit, but as soon as they are peacefully occupied with looking at the old castle and discussing the plans of the artist who, by means of his art, wants to bring about some harmony between the work of man and the work of nature, the fire does erupt. And the Princess, her fears increased by her memory of the uncle's description of the earlier fire, does the wrong thing by wishing to return to the town. She makes the wrong move again when the tiger appears and she tries to force her horse back up to the castle. Except for the owners of the wild animals, everybody acts, or plans to act, in precisely the wrong and most harmful way. The irony underlying the description of all these human actions is very striking,

[163]

particularly in comparison with the unironic and loving treatment of the gypsy family that owns the animals. Another interesting contrast, treated with irony by the author but not even felt as a contrast by the characters, is that between the Prince and the simple people. In this story, the simple people have all the wisdom, faith and love which the more refined characters lack, although they are by no means unsympathetically treated. The story itself is the vehicle of this irony, the causes of which will be shortly discussed.

Seen from the angle of "man versus nature" or "nature versus man," the author's irony, too, is remarkable. The visitors wanted to see to what extent the artist might create harmony between what had been man-made and what had been covered over by nature's vital growth. At the very moment when man, i.e., the artist, interferes with this natural process, the "wild" animals appear—only to be tamed by man, in turn. Fire, the worst of nature's forces, had overcome the prudence of man and made the escape of the animals possible. Thus the "great struggle" between man and nature is constantly evident, sometimes giving the victory to man, sometimes to nature. The fact that, in the story, man wins in the end has nothing to do with man's greater power, but rather with the nearness to nature of these simple people. If they were not so close to nature, they could not tame it—this is the ultimate irony of the story. It is not the mighty who tame the grim lion, but the little boy with his flute and his song.

The biblical references related to these three simple people form a particularly fitting setting for them. In the simplicity of the Old Testament words and images, such miracles as the present one seem likely and understandable. But there is something even more fundamental involved here. These natural people have a love of "nature," i.e., the animals, which the high and mighty have lost. And the latter shoot, while the former sing. It is in the power of the simple woman to forgive Honorio for having killed her tiger because she instinctively understands the "wild animal" in Honorio himself, namely his momentarily unbridled passion for the Princess; and, by telling him to overcome his passion (*sich überwinden*), she shows herself to be superior and kinder than the killer of her animal. Every adult is put to shame by the fearless confidence of the boy who is the only "man" stronger than nature.

[164]

A symbolic analysis like the one just attempted is bound to do much harm to the story, because it intellectualizes what in the story is an aesthetic presence. Such unavoidable abstractions are especially harmful to a story every detail of which is carefully worked out by an author who manages to remain aesthetically precise despite, and for the sake of, his symbolic intent. The perfect coordination between aesthetic detail and symbolic meaning produces in every word and image a tension and vibration which cannot be rendered by analysis.

V The Man of Fifty Years

In this very sketchy presentation of Goethe's life and work, a lengthy discussion of the sequel to *Wilhelm Meister's Appenticeship*, namely *Wilhelm Meister's Years of Wandering* has no place. Of all of Goethe's major productions it is, in my opinion, the least appealing to the modern mind. Its problems are not ours, and even the scope of the conversations and issues may appear tedious to anyone who is not closely familiar with Goethe's work and therefore willing to inquire more deeply into his thought. I do not mean to imply that it is a worthless piece of writing, but I simply feel that it has no place in an introductory study such as this one.

Quite aside from many personal adventures and aberrations which occur in this book, the main themes of the novel concern two major realms of human endeavor and attitude: the problem of education, often through art, but also through the experiences of life; and the idea of resignation, of giving up what one loves best and growing through this experience. Nowhere else, except perhaps in *Iphigenie*, has Goethe so carefully explored the possibilities of growth through resignation. It would be wrong, however, to consider this attitude the single fundamental "wisdom" Goethe meant to convey. Both themes are undoubtedly major concerns of his mature years, but it does not follow that he has forgotten the passionate emotions of the human heart. The interpolated tales seem to have as their main purpose within the novel the unfolding of the errors and follies of the human heart, unmitigated by either education or resignation.

I would like to introduce one of these inserted tales, in order to show in which way the old Goethe's style of storytelling developed. *The Man of Fifty Years* is a remarkable story. It is carefully fitted into the mainstream of the novel by a number of devices: it starts in Book II, chapter 3—i.e., somewhere near the center of the novel, and occupies three chapters, which are numbered not according to its own divisions, but rather to those of the novel itself. Technically, this fact clearly indicates the position which the tale occupies within the larger context. While it runs, to all appearance, its independent course, the Baroness of the tale, in an hour of need, turns for help to one of the most important characters in the novel, the wise woman Makarie who holds all characters of the novel together by a bond of loving sympathy. Whereas, when first mentioned in the tale, she is only a shadowy figure, she turns out in the end to have been in contact with the Baroness throughout the second half of the tale and to have been able, through her letters, to make each character of the tale aware of his or her true situation by holding up, as it were, a mirror which shows his own truth to each person. Also, the Baroness' daughter, Hilarie, who is in some ways the heroine of the tale, belongs to Makarie's immediate environment.

The tale itself is fairly long and moves at a contemplative pace—with the exception of several exciting, very emotional high points which give the tale its poignancy. The story is simple enough: The man of fifty years, brother of the Baroness, is loved by his young niece Hilarie, who was promised to his son Flavio. But Flavio is in love with a lovely young widow and, therefore, anxious for his father to marry the young girl. The father, although aware of his advanced age, needs little persuasion. However, as the bridal arrangements are almost completed, Flavio appears in the castle in great disarray and distress caused by the refusal of the widow to marry him. At this precise moment, Hilarie discovers her love for the son rather than the father, a love furthered by Flavio's prolonged stay at the castle. When the father finally arrives, he has no choice but to give up Hilarie. We may assume—without being absolutely certain—that the young couple will marry one day and that the Major will marry the widow.

Shorn of its rich artistry, the story seems very simple. But the storyteller is not a simple man; in fact, he is an author of consummate skill. In the first place, he knows exactly how to create suspense, in the characters as well as in the reader. When the Major first visits Hilarie and her mother, the Baroness tells him immediately that their plan to unite Flavio and Hilarie will not work out since Hilarie has lost her heart to someone else. At this moment, Hilarie interrupts the conversation by entering with the breakfast, and both the Major and the reader are left in suspense as to who this man might be. With the fine tact of an experienced storyteller, Goethe tells us that the Major is "almost jealous" of the unknown lover and does not even notice that each dish is one of his own favorites and prepared in the way he likes it best. On the contrary, he feels that the breakfast does not taste good; and the songs Hilarie sings afterwards leave him cold. He does not realize that he is himself the "someone else."

It is this detailed description of the Major's reaction which immediately catches our attention. There is a truth in this reaction whose knowledge seems to stem from the author's vast experience. At every point in the tale, we encounter accurate details. And since the tale is crowded with changing emotions, we are delighted to watch, over and over again, a great observer of the human heart expose its strange reactions which are quite unknown to the characters themselves. There is great finesse in these observations, which are anything but trivial. At every turn, a new emotional situation develops, and each one is captured with complete mastery of detail. Goethe's tale-telling is no longer in need of symbolism or even of an "unusual event." However, he does not present the psychological facts, but transforms them immediately into gestures and attitudes. The words which the characters speak are generally not the foremost expression of their feelings, in contrast to their "moods" and "behavior", which Goethe captures in their most delicate nuances.

Another outstanding authorial device consists in the presentation of "dramatic moments." Two of them constitute true turning-points in the action. The first occurs after Flavio's confused and desperate appearance in the castle.

Hilarie stepped forward, he shook hands with her—Greetings, dear sister—that touched her heart. He held on to her hand, they looked at each other—the loveliest couple, contrasting beautifully. The young man's black, shining eyes corresponded to the dark tousled hair; by contrast, she stood still—apparently heavenly in her stillness. But to the shattering event of his home-coming was added a prophetic present. He called her sister—her inmost being was upset.[2]

This is the precise moment when she realizes her error of having mistaken the father for the son.

The second highlight is, if possible, even more dramatic. There had been a flood followed by a sudden frost. Ice-skating became the young couple's favorite pastime. The Major, not aware of developments at home, had visited some of his other estates. It is night, the moon shines brightly, and the young couple enjoys the skating, when suddenly they feel encircled by a man skating around them.

With some composure they tried to gain the shade, In the pale light of the moon, that man skated toward them, He stood closely before them, it was impossible to mistake him for anyone but the father.

Hilarie, stopping, lost her balance and fell to the ground. Flavio immediately fell on his knee, took her head in his lap. She hid her face, she did not know what had happened to her. —"I will get a sled," the Major says.[3]

When the Major returns with a sled, the young couple is gone, and the full truth hits him with great force.

I will forgo a discussion of the more meditative parts of the tale. While the topics of these meditations, generally presented in the form of a dialogue, have immediate relevance to the main events, they nevertheless have the effect of slowing down the pace of the action. This, however, is not simply an idiosyncrasy of the author, but rather a technique of storytelling, intended, as we have seen in *Elective Affinities*, as a retardation of a plot which, in its dramatic moments, tends to further the action precipitously. Life, as Goethe saw it, contains both the dramatic and the meditative elements. Most "drama" in human life is interrupted by long moments of waiting, and solutions are not as easily found as some tales might make us believe. Goethe is a realist when he interrupts the rapid flow of passions—but he is simultaneously the storyteller who keeps us in suspense.

Altogether, *The Man of Fifty Years* shows the great advance Goethe's technique of storytelling has made. Goethe presents not so much an "event," as the reactions of all the participants to the event. Not for a second is the reader unaware of the true emotions of the characters which the observant author puts before him. This indicates a new phase in the development of Goethe's tales, his final and delicate understanding of motivation and reaction.

CHAPTER 8

Faust Parts I and II

IN view of Goethe's general acceptance of the changeability and transience of life, it is interesting to realize that he must also have suffered from these truths felt by him to be unalterable. His most daring, as well as most influential, work, *Faust,* begun in the early 1770's and finished only a few months before his death, testifies to the existence of this suffering. Faust, the hero, and *Faust,* the drama, indicate a knowledge not only of the existence of transience in every moment of our lives, but also of the human tragedy resulting from this lack of stability.

The work overcomes the problem of transience by moving within the realm of myth, where human failures and weaknesses, as well as achievements and greatness, are seen outside of time and presented as poetic rather than realistic truth, in the one mode given to man, where he might feel secure from the passing of time and the changing of forms. What Goethe achieved in *Faust* is the transformation of changing situations into the lasting realm of art. He does not deny the change of everything existing —on the contrary, he presents every change [1] in the work as change. But precisely by presenting it as change he gives to the passing moment its glorification and its permanence in poetry.

In Goethe's œuvre, Faust occupies a very special place. As we know from *Wilhelm Meister* and *Iphigenie,* the poet often first conceived of a work, without being able to write it immediately in what he considered its final form. Even some poems, such as *An den Mond,* underwent several metamorphoses before Goethe was satisfied with the outcome. The spontaneity of the conception and the careful elaboration of the final form were, for Goethe, often separate functions. And as he despaired of finding that final form, he left the portions of the earlier versions in his drawer in the remote hope of finishing them one day. As the years went by, his taste and his outlook on many problems changed, and so the original was changed and given a final form according to the new insights of a later period. There have always been critics who preferred the first spontaneous, youthful version of Goethe's works. Such a critical stand is not really open to discussions because it depends entirely on personal taste.

With regard to *Faust* I prefer to take the opposite stand. Goethe did not consider *Faust* completed until a year before his death when he locked it away to resist the temptation of further changes. I do not believe that we have a right to accept the work on any other basis than this judgment of the author himself. Whereas it is true that Goethe worked on *Faust*, with long interruptions, for over sixty years, it is equally true that, for the last thirty years of this span, he had a definite vision of what he wanted to achieve, and faithfully adhered to it. We have a few sketches of scenes he did not carry out, but on the whole he faithfully elaborated on the unified vision he had conceived around the turn of the century. The unity of the work, then, is guaranteed by this vision, as well as by its manifestation in the final form of 1831.

What could attract an enlightened, forward-looking, scientifically oriented mind such as Goethe's to an old Christian legend in which a man makes a pact with the devil to acquire knowledge, power and wealth, but who will never enjoy them because he knows he has forfeited his soul and cannot be redeemed? Whatever Goethe's religious beliefs, there was no room in his thinking for the existence of Hell, the devil and eternal damnation. Nevertheless, he felt so strongly attracted to the legend which he had seen as a child in the form of a puppet-play that he had to transform it into his own, radically modern version. The idea of a human being who can overcome many of the limitations of ordinary man by having "magic" means at his disposal is, indeed, attractive to the modern mind. It was also a poetic challenge, since for the presentation of the life of a superman poetic means had to be found appropriate to, and expressive of, a truly modern, isolated, and alienated individual's earthly existence. That the work grew from a relatively simple, although tragic, love-story into the universal story of modern man was inevitable once Goethe realized the full potential of his material. And that he managed to hold this story strictly within the limits of poetic expression is his great achievement. The work makes sense only inasmuch as it *is* poetic expression—it would not only fall flat if it were told in prose, but it would essentially cease to make sense.

The fundamental poetic technique of the work is one that had long existed and became generally acceptable again only at a much later date: *Faust* consists of a series of dramatic scenes which, although their sequence could hardly be altered, gives—upon first reading—the misleading impression of being arbitrary. However, the episodes are not only held together by the necessities of the plot; they are, in a much more essential way, connected by a large number of symbolic devices which give structural unity to the work. There are many recurring symbols or symbolic images, as, for instance, the alternation of day and night as a symbol of the natural rhythm of waking and sleeping, of activity and rest, etc., or gold as a symbol of man's greed and destructiveness.

Furthermore there is a style of language characteristic—or perhaps better: symbolic—of each character. Faust's language is distinguished by a high-flown poetic style, enriched by beautiful nature imagery and strongly emotional overtones. By contrast, Mephistopheles, the devil of the work, likes four-letter words, and his tone is cold, cynical, "realistic." He likes to use images of animals which are mostly chosen for their repulsiveness to man.

Another symbolic device consists in the meters and rhymes in which the work is written. A great variety of meters are consciously used to indicate moods, characters, and events. The knowing reader will find the meaning of an individual passage by comparing its meter to the use of an identical one in other passages. Thus the reader is called upon to read with great attention to detail a work which, without such careful reading, may appear bewildering in its richness of incident and character.

The fundamental and tragic theme of the work is Faust's awareness of the instability of every earthly thing, event, thought and feeling. He is searching for absolutes and finds that they do not exist. It becomes clear to the reader that this is in the nature of life,[2] but Faust never accepts this truth and continues his search despite his repeated failures. His life thus falls into a rhythm of illusions about the offerings of life and disappointments when they prove to be transitory. This is not an intellectual experience, but a much more deep-seated emotional one. His whole existence is shattered by each new disillusionment, although his innate vitality will drive him on to a new experience whose disillusioning character he will gradually discover.

The rhythm of Faust's life expresses itself not only in the dualism between illusion and disillusionment; the entire work is characterized by a polarity between opposing forces which are not only contradictory but often paradoxical. Neither one of these opposites will ever defeat the other—their essential truth consists in the fact that they co-exist in contradiction to each other. To Faust's thinking, the most fundamental opposing forces in man are body and mind. Man is caught in the struggle between them, which will be resolved only after his death when the angels carrying his "immortal part" upward will sing:

> Kein Engel trennte   No angel can divide
> Geeinte Zwienatur   Dual self made one;
> Die ewige Liebe nur   Eternal love alone
> Vermag's zu scheiden.   Can separate this.

(Passage, p. 407, slightly revised)

Early in the play, Faust recognizes the fact that he has "two souls," which he describes as spiritual and earthly. This dichotomy between mind and body is presented as the all-pervasive dualism which causes man's suffering and despair.

On one of the levels on which the play must be read, this dualism is symbolized and, as it were, externalized by the very characters of Faust and Mephistopheles. If Faust, in this particular context, represents the searching and frustrated human mind, Mephistopheles clearly takes the part of the body. In the case of Faust's love of Margaret, the devil is not only the tempter, but, even more so, the "realist" who points ironically and devastatingly to Faust's physical desire which, for Mephistopheles, constitutes the essence of human love. In this particular instance, Faust, although, of course, succumbing to the physical attraction and thereby ruining the beloved, simultaneously realizes that his love for the girl is much more than an attraction of the moment. And while Margaret, in the logic of the play, must die, Faust preserves his love until he meets her again after his death when she will lead him "upward."

Faust and Mephistopheles also are true opposites on many other levels. One of the important contrasts is that between Faust's seriousness and Mephistopheles' irony. In fact, this irony, one of the devil's most attractive features, is, at times, simply a comic device making the reader laugh when he might have been moved —and at times even bored—by Faust's high flights. But more often than not, this irony is serious, that is, the author uses Mephistopheles' "realistic" viewpoint to express the duality pervading all life, all intellectual issues, all emotions and all events. Thus everything in the play is simultaneously taken seriously by Faust and mocked by the devil. And only if we accept both aspects as being equally true and relevant can we begin to understand the author's intention. The rhythm of day and night, which symbolically reflects the rhythm of Faust's life, also reflects the rhythm of life—biological and physical, plant and animal—in general, it is the essential characteristic of life on this earth which, by its very nature, must be considered both with seriousness and irony, because its powerful presence and its short duration are equally strong experiences.

That both the dualism of life, its bright and dark side as well as the instability of everything existing are the central concerns of the work is first made clear in the "Prologue in Heaven" during which the angels, praising God's creation, devote one stanza of their song to the alternation of day and night, and to the storms and the seemingly senseless motions they produce. The angels can turn their faces from this disturbing sight to the contemplation of God's "gentle day," but Faust is forced to face both the dualism of life and the lack of permanence, which cause him to despair. As Mephistopheles offers him the joys of this world, Faust curses every human event and situation that, misleadingly, presuppose stability and would therefore require daily care. Instead, Faust suggests to the devil a bet in which he promises never to rest, but rather to run from one empty moment to the next. It is a desperate bet, but Faust adheres to it throughout his life, thereby making the devil procure for him whatever empty pleasures he may be able to provide. That, in reality, Faust's life, although lonely and guilt-ridden, is in a subtle way more meaningful than he could anticipate at the moment of signing the pact, is seen throughout the work.

The moment of the bet marks the end of Faust's academic

[*173*]

career, whose emptiness he has learned to loathe. Instead, he will go out into life to experience love, nature, and art. And whereas none of these important realms of human experience will "last" in Faust's sense, they nevertheless will fill his life with something other than total emptiness. Faust's progress through life will be characterized by loss and guilt, but his vitality carries him from one situation to the next with an ever new and youthful impulse. Thus, while he keeps his pact with the devil in a literal sense and his desperate attitude toward life does not change, he learns to live with the eternal fickleness of life which caused his initial despair.

The pact, however, is the ultimate cause of Faust's isolation. As long as he works in his study, he has at least an assistant, Wagner, a funny caricature of a scholar. But the more he becomes tied to Mephistopheles, the more he will be isolated. Certainly, he falls in love with Margaret, but, from the start, the girl's life is doomed. Faust knows that he is the intruder into a life protected by religion and strict bourgeois upbringing, and that no vow of eternal love can undo the harm he does by seducing her. But he causes her ruin despite his own awareness of the situation and despite his guilt-feelings. The great simplicity of the girl strongly contrasts with Faust's own complex character and emphasizes the guilt that the knowing and mature man must feel when faced with her profound innocence.

Throughout the rest of the work Faust does not form a personal and human relationship. At the Emperor's court, to which Mephistopheles takes him after Margaret's death, he merely plays the role of the Court Necromancer, which is also his role when subsequently he helps the Emperor in winning a battle over the Counter-Emperor. And the entourage of the Emperor does not have any endearing human quality. His relationship to Helen of Troy is not in the order of a purely human relationship. And in the last act of the play when, owning his own land, he is surrounded by "magic" helpers, they destroy the only human beings inhabiting the land: an old couple, Philemon and Baucis, who had lived on it for many years, and a guest to whom they had offered hospitality.

In this short summary of Faust's associations with other human beings nothing is omitted. After the death of Margaret, who is executed because she has killed their child, there is no other human bond and Faust's only intercourse, aside from his ties to the devil, is with spirits or mythological figures. I am not distinguishing here between spirits and mythological figures, as all of them are figments of the imagination, taken by Goethe from various realms of mythology, whether Greek or Christian. The Christian mythological figures are generally called spirits, in contrast to those belonging to ancient myth. In the way they are treated in the work, however, no artistic distinction is made.

The world of magic, spirits, and mythological figures owes its existence only to a small extent to Mephistopheles. To be sure, the first "Walpurgis Night," a witches' sabbath by means of which Mephistopheles hopes to make Faust forget Margaret and her tragic fate, is indeed closely connected with the devil. It is the feast of the reawakening of spring presented as the reawakening of sex. The earlier scene "Witches Kitchen," in which Faust is rejuvenated by means of a love potion, serves the same purpose of awakening sexual desire. But in the "Walpurgis Night" Faust has a vision of Margaret with a red line around her neck, symbolizing her execution; and he thereby evades the lure of the naked witch with whom he is dancing. Once again, as throughout the play, his spiritual self overcomes his physical desire.

Most spirits in the play—and there are many—exist independently of Mephistopheles, although some of them may well be "distant relatives." The Earth Spirit whom Faust conjures up at the beginning was originally (i.e., in the first version of the play) intended to have sent Mephistopheles to Faust. And whatever their relationship in the final version, they are undoubtedly akin because of their close connection with the earth. This is also partly true for Homunculus, the little man in the test-tube, created by Wagner, who would not have come to life without the appearence of the devil.

But Homunculus is more spirit than matter, and it is, therefore, left to him to find a means of bringing Faust back from a deep paralysis into which the beauty of Helen of Troy has thrown him. And since he is a mind-reader, he knows that Faust is dreaming of Leda, Helen's mother, as she is visited by the swan. Homunculus suggests that they all go off to a classical Walpurgis Night in which the mythological figures of early antiquity appear, not more beautiful than the earlier witches, but considerably more poised and less sexed. Above all, they are much older than Mephistopheles and mock him freely. In the beautiful myth of that Walpurgis Night, Faust finds Helen, Homunculus is "born" to be a man, Mephistopheles finds a mythological shape enabling him to serve Helen, and Eros, the mighty god of universal love, reigns supreme.

During this glorification of the powers of nature (all of which are represented as mythological figures) and for the period of this mythological moment, time stands still; the long development of man from the most primitive form of life to his present shape is seen as if transience did not matter: the space is vast and open, cause and effect are irrelevant and Faust finds happiness. However, since this experience takes place in the realm of mythology, not in "real" life, it has no bearing on the pact.

The same is true for Act III of *Faust II*, where Faust leads a mythological life with Helen of Troy. She bears him a son, an unearthly creature, generally considered to be an allegory of poetry, who flies to Heaven like Icarus and dies in a grand fall. In his death, he calls his mother back to Hades, and Helen disappears just as she came, a mythological figure who is alive to those who call her to life, like Faust, but whose appearance, depending entirely on the momentary call of an earthly man, is not to be retained in any earthly life.

When he is first asked by the Emperor to produce Paris and Helen of Troy, Faust, being at a loss about how to find them, accepts Mephistopheles' advice to go to the "Mothers." This is a trip into "Nothingness" during which Faust finds the "Mothers" surrounded by the shadowy figures representing the far-distant mythological past. The Mothers represent, as it were, the memory of mankind from which Faust can extract the shade of Helen. The Mothers myth, along with certain other of the most important figures in the work, is Goethe's own invention.

To fulfill his life, Faust once more has to savor its bitterness; he will have to become guilty again and re-experience its illusory character. From the viewpoint of Faust's development, the catastrophe of Act V is well prepared through Act IV, which, in turn, is prepared in Act II. The Emperor's Court is shown satirically as the most shallow of human institutions. While the courtiers amuse themselves with acting a masquerade, Faust and the devil not only produce false gold, but also print the first paper money,

[176]

based on the patently false assumption that there are surely rich treasures in the ground.

Similarly, in Act IV Faust and Mephistopheles help the Emperor win a battle against an Anti-Emperor by means of some uncanny helpers taken from the Bible but transformed into blasphemous caricatures of the biblical figures, and by creating a flood which is no real flood but which, nonetheless, repels the enemy troops. This hollow "victory" procures for Faust a piece of land near the ocean (the Netherlands), where Act V will take place. The beginning of this act calls the Margaret scenes to mind. The old couple's innocence, and Faust's greed, which causes their death, are, on the level of old age, what Margaret was in Faust's youth. But more than that: after the allegorical figure of Care blinds him, he has a vision of what he would like to do with the land he has reclaimed from the ocean. It is a precarious piece of land, and he wishes people to live on it precariously. But while he dreams of a productive future and listens to the sound of spades, obeying, as he believes, his orders to dig the last canal, he is under another delusion: in reality the spades are digging his grave.

Thus Faust dies winning his bet because, even if his last dream had come true, it would not have altered his unstable life. Mephistopheles does not get his soul which, in a last poetic and hymnic scene, is carried upward toward a sphere of love.

In this final scene we are faced with the Christian mythology of the redemption of the soul. The inevitable question the reader will ask himself at this moment is one that has disturbed many critics: how can a man be saved—against the logic of the legend— who has done a great deal of wrong and no real good, who has spent his life in selfish greed, who has lacked humility, has foresworn all care of others and never served anyone but himself, a man, moreover, who could not appreciate the joys offered to him because he was forever running after new experience. Goethe actually accumulates instances of Faust's guilt both in the Gretchen tragedy and in that of the old couple.

The only conceivable answer must be that the kind of redemption presented in the last scene has nothing to do with the problem of good and evil. Faust is obviously "saved" despite his evil deeds and without any form of repentence. The work considers the existence of evil as an unavoidable and necessary part of life. This does not mean that evil is easily excused; on the contrary, the emphasis on its existence and its terror is great. But it does mean that the work is directed toward life as such where moral problems are only a small part of a far greater whole. The fleeting quality of time, the illusion of stability, the continual change of everything living, the puzzle of a human mind seated in an animal body—these are the themes of the work, whose unity comes about through the fact that its hero is, himself, the central symbol of life in all these aspects.

Redemption, then, means continuation rather than salvation. There is, gently superimposed on this modern work, the neo-Platonic view familiar from Goethe's poetry which explains the conflict between body and mind. The world-soul, whose creative act is to manifest itself in "matter," is present in everything created and in man more than in any other thing. Man's own creativity is a mirror of the over-all creativity of life; but he is tied to his body while simultaneously conscious of this tie, and his great desire to join the world-soul again in a pure, spiritual state cannot be fulfilled in life—it happens only after death when the mind is freed from the body.

By a fortunate coincidence, on which Goethe could freely draw, this myth of the soul's separation from, and return to, the world-soul allows, as we have seen, free rein to his modern, scientific interpretation of life. The development of life from the smallest particle to the complex being, man, fits without contradition into the old myth. It would be wrong to say that *Faust* is poised between an old belief and a modern view of the world. The scale tips strongly toward the modern side, not only with regard to Faust's character and the philosophic implications of the play, but also with regard to its symbolic form. However, the old faith is still there, not so much as a religious belief but rather as a poetic vision. The last scene, with its Christian mythology and its very un-Christian salvation, is the clearest proof of Goethe's ever-present faith in the world-soul which animates and sustains all life.

Myth, as we have seen, is the mode of the entire work; it is the realm in which all characters move and all actions occur. The Faust legend itself is elevated into the myth of modern man; and the Christian devil is transformed into the myth of earthiness. The Earth-Spirit, Goethe's own invention, mythologically encompasses the sum of human life on earth. There are spirits—the so-called neutral spirits created by the Renaissance thinkers—whose specific purpose is to "fulfill" the hierarchy of existence. And there are ancient creatures, low and high, wise and silly, just as there are sensuous and reckless witches. The various young Faust figures, Homunculus, Euphorion, Lynceus (who owe their literary existence to alchemical or ancient legends), are all embedded in the mythological texture of the play. Even the empty courtiers turn into mythological characters, as they act out a masquerade at the Emperor's Court. The world of the play is so essentially mythological that the reader forgets the "real" or "legendary" origin of a character and understands the whole to be poetic reality. This interpretation of the work as a grand myth quite naturally includes the Christian figures and symbols as well as the many biblical quotations. They, too, contribute to the myth of modern, biologically conditioned man who, dissatisfied with his fragmentary knowledge of life, decides to find answers for his questions not in the books he has learned to despise but in the richness and elusiveness of life on earth.

CHAPTER 9

Conclusion

IT can be argued that, aside from several poems, Goethe never wrote a "perfect" work of art. His mind was, like Faust's, never satisfied with one complete manifestation. Shakespeare, in *King Lear*, or Milton, in *Paradise Lost* abandoned themselves more completely to their works than Goethe, who held his innermost self back, perhaps in the fear of losing himself too completely. The poetic distance he creates, which is his great achievement, is also his limitation. The reader feels this distance as a restraint imposed on him by an author who values his aloofness more than his abandonment. Do we know the author when we read his works? The answer is that we know him only partially and that he defends his privacy as his strongest asset.

The reader's sense of never quite penetrating into the author's mind is partly caused by Goethe's avoidance of abstract thought. He is not a writer who expresses ideas but a poet who thinks in images. As long as the reader is willing to follow the author's visual associations, he will be greatly rewarded. Read as an author of ideas, Goethe will soon appear trivial.

Several qualities of his mind stand out: the first is his sensitive understanding of human situations and the human heart. Humaneness on every level of existence is his constant concern, and any violation of this attitude is anathema to him. His equally strong sensitivity to nature and all its phenomena has been discussed at sufficient length.

Another basic characteristic is his almost unlimited open-mindedness to *all* phenomena occurring in human and natural life. This includes, among many other features, his interest in all forms of art.[1] It also includes a cosmopolitanism which is a heritage of eighteenth-century attitudes, but is generally lost in Germany during the Napoleonic Wars. If Goethe was not a friend of the French Revolution, he was also not a friend of the

Prussian nationalism which infected the Romantic writers. For him, to meet Napoleon meant to meet a great man. Patriotism did not enter into the problem. But his younger friends could not easily forgive this attitude. In a similar way, Beethoven, the rebel, could not forgive him that he bowed to aristocracy. But, in contrast to the composer, Goethe had spent his life in aristocratic circles and behaved according to traditional etiquette.

It seems fairly clear that those of the younger generation who criticized him did so in reaction to their own overawed respect and reverence. In Germany he reigned not only as her greatest poet, but as a guide to taste and art appreciation. And yet, from our own perspective, we can easily see the limits of his taste and his aesthetic judgment. Thus, the greatest poets of the younger generation, namely Hölderlin and Kleist—both urgently in need of support from him—were not recognized by him. Goethe was kind, but condescending to both and forgot them all too easily.

The controversy around Goethe which I mentioned in the beginning is thus not due entirely to modern re-appraisal. It is, ultimately, based on Goethe's own behavior. To what an extent our criticism of the author's behavior should overshadow our appreciation of his œuvre is up to the individual to decide. I have not concealed his flaws, although they do not seem to me to be of urgent interest. His works, however, I consider important, original, in part very beautiful, and in many ways extremely "modern." I hope to have shown how many-sided his talents and his interests were, and how much broader than those of his Romantic successors, both inside and outside of Germany.

It remains for us to offer a brief sketch of the enormous influence Goethe exercised. There is, first of all, the German school system, which absorbed and appropriated him. Nobody educated in it until very recently could ever quite rid himself of the impression that Germany had produced one demi-god, whom no one else, except perhaps Dante and Shakespeare, could match. Since every German author born after Goethe went through the German school system, they all were brought up with an image they did not help to shape. Only those few minds who, in the course of their lives, created their own image of the author could come up with anything approaching originality. Thomas Mann's satiric re-creation of Goethe in his novel *Lotte in Weimar* is perhaps the most interesting because it helps much to deflate the myth so carefully preserved in German thinking. Most contemporaries of Thomas Mann still believed in the myth. They imitated either his style (Hesse), his appearance (Hauptmann), or his poetic language (Hofmannsthal). I have omitted earlier generations who lived almost too close to Goethe to be able to shake off his influence on their style, their thinking, their attitudes toward life.

In foreign countries, too, he was greatly admired. During his life, visitors streamed to Weimar, among them Mme de Stäel, who wrote of him: "Nothing troubles the power of his mind; and even the inconvenient parts of his character, ill humor, embarrassment, constraint, pass like clouds at the bottom of the mountain on whose summit his genius is placed." [2] His works were translated into many languages. To what an extent they were actually read, remains an open question. But imitations are frequent, and he is praised throughout the nineteenth century in many tongues. Of all of his works, *Faust* made undoubtedly the greatest impression. Its literary reception, from Byron's *Manfred* to Bulgakov's *The Master and Margarita* (1938), is too vast in scope to be discussed here. Thomas Mann's *Doktor Faustus* (1947) is the latest, and perhaps also last, of these works inspired by Goethe—although it uses the folk-book more than Goethe's drama.

Aside from the strictly literary influences felt in many countries and languages, Goethe's poetic language has held a great fascination for composers, who early took hold of his poetry. Starting with his friend Zelter, and continuing with Loewe, Schubert, Schumann, and Wolf, lieder were composed in unheard-of quantity; The compositions involving Faust themes are equally numerous. Aside from at least fourteen full-length operas, there are a large number of choral works, the greatest of which is probably Gustav Mahlers' Eighth Symphony, whose choral text is the last scene of *Faust II*.

Performances of Goethe's plays are not as frequent now as they were in the nineteenth and the early part of the twentieth century; but they are still in every municipal theater's repertory. His name is a legend wherever you turn, and I doubt that the present critical attitude will change this. Goethe himself may have contributed to the creation of this legend, and his contemporary admirers certainly did. But legends have a long life, and his principal merit, namely to have written the works discussed in this book—and many others besides—is not legend, but a lively reality, which will continue to fascinate the minds of modern readers both in Germany and abroad.

Notes and References

Preface

1. In 1949, at the time when Goethe's two hundredth anniversary was celebrated, a number of new books about him were published. The most important is Emil Staiger's *Goethe*, in 3 volumes, a study that was lavishly praised at the time of publication, but seems, from our present point of view, partly frozen in the earlier superannuated tradition.

2. Shakespeare, e.g., had been considered "barbaric" until he was "rediscovered" in the late eighteenth century.

Chapter One

1. See on the "demonic" below (Ch. III, note 33) p. 190.

2. See below p. 25.

3. Much later Goethe composed from these particular diaries two autobiographical works, called *The Campaign in France* (1822) and *The Siege of Mainz* (1823). They are very interesting, observant accounts of the military campaigns against the French, on which Goethe had to accompany his Duke.

4. *Of My Life: Fiction and Truth*. The three first books were published in 1814; the last book was finished before Goethe died, but published only after his death. *The Italian Journey* was published in 1817.

5. In *Fiction and Truth*, Part II, Book 7, (HA IX, 283).

6. See for this statement the brilliant introduction (not available in English) by Erich Trunz to the Autobiography in the so-called "Hamburger Ausgabe." Trunz himself gives an excellent analysis of the work, but points out the lack of an exhaustive study. He emphasizes the fact that it is the first autobiography written with a sense of history. This gives the work its large scope. Trunz's edition will be quoted as HA.

7. Not only is the work written from old notes, personal memories and the replies of old friends to many queries, but it was never meant to be "historical truth." Much of what Goethe includes is actual fact, but much is due to his desire to give the work artistic shape. For him the fictions existing in the work are poetic truth, for they make the often incoherent historical truth understandable and real.

8. He speaks of conciseness of form just a few pages prior to the above quotation.

9. In German it does not sound well to start a word with the con-

sonant with which the previous word has ended: un*d D*ichtung is a sound combination Goethe carefully avoided.

10. The main passage on French literature is in Part III, Book 11. (HA, IX, 483 ff).

11. See my article: "Repeated Mirror Reflections: The Technique of Goethe's Novels." *Studies in Romanticism I* (1962), 154–174.

12. "The New Paris" in Part I, Book 2.

13. See Hans Rudolf Vaget: *Dilettantismus und Meisterschaft. Zum Problem des Dilettantismus bei Goethe: Praxis, Theorie, Zeitkritik* (Munich, Winkler, 1971.)

14. See below p. 148 ff.

Chapter Two

1. From a fragment, called *Nature*, written in 1783.

2. Goethe had just started to do some anatomical studies. See below p. 000.

3. In HA, XIII, 107.

4. This edition is called *Ausgabe letzter Hand.* Some parts of it were not published until after Goethe's death.

5. The Hamburg edition. See Ch. I, note 6.

6. The German word for shape is *Form.* We can easily distinguish, by means of their form, between a maple and an oak leaf. They are characteristic and never interchangeable. Goethe often uses another word for shape, and above all for "to shape." The verb is "bilden," derived from "Bild" (image). Goethe uses it to indicate the creative force of nature. The word "Bildung," derived from "bilden," furthermore means the formation, i.e. the education, of man. Goethe often applied his philosophy of the formative powers of nature to human development.

7. "There is always something stiff and inflexible about them" (i.e., the physical sciences), HA, XIII, 492.

8. See Chapter VIII.

9. See above, p. 41. Metamorphosis is simply the original Greek term for what was translated, in Latin, as transformation.

10. "Schicksal der Handscrift," HA, XIII, 102–105.

11. *Ibid.*, 105–112.

12. For a discussion of the poem see below p. 69.

13. Printed only in *Morphology I*, 1820. See HA, XIII, 184–196.

14. On polarity and growth see Goethe's letter to the Chancellor von Müller, in HA, XIII, 48.

15. See Goethe's description of chemical reactions to Lacmus paper.

16. See "Colorful Shades" (*Farbige Schatten*) in HA, XIII, 345–350, which is part of the chapter on physiological colors.

17. Luke Howard; *"Essay on Modification of Clouds."* (London, 1805).

18. See Ernst Loeb; *Die Symbolik des Wasserzyklus bei Goethe.* (Paderborn, 1967).

Chapter Three

1. In the final edition of his works, Goethe himself divided his poems—at least a large portion thereof—according to their poetic form.

2. Berlin, 1922.

3. The "Knittelvers" is a German verse used mainly in the sixteenth century by the "Meistersinger." It has four feet, with regular accents on the stressed syllables, but an irregular number of unaccented syllables. It is used in large portions of *Faust*.

4. Goethe's early poem to his grandparent has solemn Alexandrine lines, whereas a poem on Christ's trip to hell is written in a four-foot iambic meter.

5. Pindar wrote what in Greek is called Hymns but in English odes. Klopstock, who tried to imitate Pindar and whom Goethe followed, called his Pindaric poems Odes. In Goethe's works, they are often referred to as Hymns, but since they are in no way Church Hymns, I will call them Odes.

6. The first and fourth line of stanza one are identical.

7. As originally published (*Musenalmanach*, 1774) it was divided among two characters: Fatema, wife of Mohamet, and Ali, his father-in-law. Underscoring the unity of the work, Goethe pulled it together in subsequent editions, making it more mysterious by omitting any direct reference to Mahomet except for the title.

8. Goethe considered as allegorical any image that had a rational and simple relationship to the object it is compared to. By contrast, a symbol, for him, was a more complex image, not necessarily "rational," but rather comprehensive and often mysterious and difficult to understand.

9. See e.g. *Wilhelm Meister's Years of Wandering*.

10. For instance, in the second stanza before the last: "bienensingenden," "honiglallenden," etc.

11. Kronos is, of course, the father of Zeus; but his name was always confused with Chronos, meaning Time.

12. For a discussion of this poem see below p. 61 f.

13. In German, a line-ending is considered masculine when the accent falls on the last syllable, and feminine when the last accented syllable is followed by a non-accented syllable: Fáss (masc.), Vátèr (fem.)

14. Some scholars maintain that the longer version was written by

Charlotte von Stein. The poem gains greatly in depth, however, if it is not considered to be a lament over lost love.

15. *The Roman Elegies* were a great favorite of Schiller's, who, in his *Letters on Esthetic Education,* formulated his own idea that art is a function of the "play instinct" (*Spieltrieb*) in man, and that, in perfect art, the parts of a work are held together in the perfect balance between forces with which the author seems to be playing.

16. Goethe wrote *Hermann and Dorothea* in hexameters, and many satirical distichs and "Xenien" in the elegiac meter.

17. See on Howard, Ch. II, p. 000.

18. "Divan" means Assembly but also denotes a collection of poetry.

19. The titles of the twelve "books" that make up the work are as follows: Book of the Bard, Book Hafis, Book of Love, Book of Musings, Book of Anger, Book of Sayings, Book Timur, Book Suleika, Book of the Cup-Bearer, Book of the Parsee, Book of Paradise.

20. See below p. 76.

21. These poems were written by Marianne von Willemer.

22. See the very informative book by Leslie Willson: *A mythical image: The Idea of India in German Romanticism* (Duke University Press, 1964).

23. E.g. in Vico, Hamann and Herder. "Poetry (i.e. the *spoken* word) is the mother tongue of mankind," is Hamann's famous phrase. In near-Eastern poetry the emphasis is always on the spoken word.

24. In another poem of the *Book Suleika* ("Tresses, hold me captive"), Hatem rhymes with Morgenröte and is obviously meant to be replaced with "Goethe."

25. For the "sound" of the sun, see the first line of the *Prologue in Heaven* in *Faust I:*

> The sun sings as it sang of old
> With brother spheres in rival sound. (Passage, p. 12)

26.   The Unlimited

> That thou can'st never end, doth make thee great,
> And that thou ne'er beginnest, is thy fate.
> Thy song is changeful as yon starry frame,
> End and beginning evermore the same;
> And what the middle bringeth, but contains
> What was at first, and what at last remains.

> Thou art of joy the true and minstrel-source,
> From thee pours wave on wave with ceaseless force.
> A mouth that's aye prepar'd to kiss,
>   A breast whence flows a loving song,

A throat that finds no draught amiss,
An open heart that knows no wrong.

And what though all the world should sink!
Hafis, with thee, along with thee
Will I contend! joy, misery,
The portion of us twain shall be!
Like thee to love, like thee to drink,—
This be my pride,—this, life to me!

Now, Song, with thine own fire be sung,—
For thou art older, thou more young!

(*Permanent Goethe*, p. 650)

27.   Holy Yearning
Tell no man, tell wise men only,
    For the world might count it madness,
Him I praise who thirsts for fire,
    Thirsts for death, and dies in gladness.

Thou wast got, and thou begattest
    In dewy love-nights long ago;
Now a stranger love shall seize thee
    When the quiet lamp burns low.

Thou art freed and lifted, taken
    From the shadow of our night,
Thou art drawn by some new passion
    Toward a nobler marriage-rite.

Distance cannot weight thee, soaring
    Where the far enchantment calls,
Till the moth, the starfire's lover,
    Drinks the light, and burns, and falls.

Die and grow! Until thou hearest
    What that word can say,
The world is dark and thou a wanderer
    Who has lost his way.

(*Permanent Goethe*, p. 643)

28.   Proem
In the Name of Him who caused Himself to be,
Creating ever from eternity,
In His name who made faith and trust and love,
The strength of things and man's activity,

Oft-named and still unfathomed mystery:
Far as thy hearing holds, far as thy sight,
Thou findest only known shapes like to His,
And soon thy spirit's furthest fire-flight
Hath store enough of symbols, likenesses.
Thou art drawn onward, sped forth joyously,
And where thou wanderest path and place grow bright;
No more thou reckonest, Time is no more for thee,
Now every footstep is Infinity. (*Permanent Goethe,* p. 644–45)

29. The distinction between world-soul and world-spirit is made in the Renaissance, from where Goethe took it over. In the hierarchy of Being, the Spirit is above the Soul, because the former is universal and the latter is individualized.

30. See above, p. 40 f.

31. In the last scene of *Faust II,* we have an indication of what Goethe had in mind. In that scene, he uses Christian symbols, whereas in the present poem the spirits are clearly taken from the world of Renaissance neo-platonic speculations.

32. No Being can dissolve into Nothing!
The Eternal works and lives in all,
Happily hold on to Being.

33. See the astrological references at the beginning of *Fiction and Truth.* What Goethe calls the "demonic" is, of course, related to the "daimon," but, in his youth, the concept of the *daimon* of this poem was not yet well developed in Goethe's thinking. Demonic, then, meant the unexplained and sometimes sinister forces that intrude into man's character and destiny. Often Goethe felt the presence of forces in man's actions and feelings that we might today explain as the unconscious, and into which his period had no insight other than that of the poets who sensed a reality behind uncanny actions or behavior. Those particular demonic forces fall, of course, into the realm of the Daimon. Any connection with evil demons must be totally avoided. avoided.

34. In the early poem "To my Goddess," he had already called Hope the older, more sedate sister of Imagination.

35. The translation of *Leiden* as "sorrow" is acceptable in the title of the book; actually, the German word is closer to "suffering."

36. See Erich Heller; "Iphigenie or the Avoidance of Tragedy" in *The Disinherited Mind* (Cambridge University Press, 1952). Latest edition New York, 1971.

37. Rainclouds, hailstorm, to sing toward, mud-path, fire-wing, flower-feet, mud of the floods.

Chapter Four

1. See *Fiction and Truth*, Part I, Ch. 3, HA, IX, 83 ff.
2. The idea is also present in Mozart's *Magic Flute*.
3. Kant's *Critique of Practical Reason*, where he discusses the "Categorical Imperative" was published in 1788. Goethe had not read Kant, but the moral demands he made were widely discussed.
4. So Tantalus's grandsons have sown curse
   On curse with full and frenzied hands! Like weeds
   That wave their wild heads, all around them strewing
   Seed thousandfold, they have begotten close-
   Kinned murderers unto their children's children
   For endless fury of retaliation!—(Passage, p. 49, 11. 968–973)
5. O let me for the first time with free heart
   Experience pure delight clasped in your arms!
   Ye gods, who walk abroad with flaming might
   And as you walk consume the heavy clouds,
   Who, graciously-severe, upon the earth
   Pour down the long-sought rain in raging streams
   Amid the thunder's voice and roar of winds,
   Yet presently resolve the shuddering dread
   Of men to blessings, changing anxious awe
   To joyous glances and loud gratitude
   When, in the raindrops on fresh-quickened leaves,
   The new sun is reflected thousandfold
   And Iris of the lovely hues with light
   Hand parts the grey veil of the final clouds,—
   O let me too, clasped in my sister's arms
   And at my dear friend's heart, enjoy and keep
   With total gratitude what you grant me!
      The curse is lifting; my heart tells me so.
   To Tartarus pass the Eumenides,
   I hear their going, and they close behind them
   The doors of bronze with far-receding thunder.
   The earth exhales refreshing fragrance and
   Invites me to its plains for full pursuit
   Of life's delights and high accomplishment.
                    (Passage, p. 60, 11. 1341–1368)
6. The biography of Tasso from which Goethe worked and which fabricated the love story with the Princess was written by Giovanni Battista Manso. For his final version of the play Goethe used the Tasso biography of the Abbate Pierantonio Serassi, published in Rome in 1785.
7. "Where does Cornelia live? Would you please show me?
   Cornelia Sersale." Friendly-wise

Some spinstress will point out the street for me
And indicate the house. I will climb higher.
The children will run after me and stare
At my wild hair and at the gloomy stranger.
I will come to the threshold. Open stands
The door, and I will step into the house—

(Passage, p. 95,, 11. 3155–62)

8. If it bechances
A letter goes astray, or a domestic
Transfers from his own service to some other,
Or if a paper gets out of his hands,
Immediately he sees design, betrayal,
And malice undermining his own fate.

(Passage, p. 12, 11. 317–322)

9. A moment later, Tasso flings this challenge at Antonio, without a trace of success.

Chapter Five

1. *Wilhelm Meister* has a sequel, *Wilhelm Meister's Years of Wandering*, written many years later and not discussed in this book except for its inserted tales. *Wilhelm Meister's Apprenticeship* can be considered complete within itself.

2. See my article on "Repeated Mirror Reflections," mentioned in Ch. I, Note 11.

3. James McPherson, who claimed he had found the original Ossian manuscript, had actually written the text himself, composing it of bits and pieces known to be old Scottish poetry. While this is one of the most famous eighteenth-century literary frauds, it is also remarkably good poetry—which is what made Goethe quote it.

4. Emilia Galotti makes her father kill her in order to preserve her virginity. Lotte also mentions *The Vicar of Wakefield* (letter of June 16) in reference to her own situation.

5. The word "romantic" occurs twice in *Werther*—a very early occurrence of the term which became common property only twenty years later.

6. See above p. 25.

7. The original version, which was entitled *Theatralische Sendung* (The Theatrical Calling) and which Goethe rewrote and enlarged between 1794 and 1796, had been copied by a Swiss friend of Goethe's, Barbara Schulthess. Her copy remained in her family and was finally published in 1911.

8. See Friedrich Schlegel's essay "Ueber Goethes *Meister*" in *Athenäum*, Vol I. (1798).

9. "Oh lass mich scheinen, bis ich werde" . . . in Book VIII, ch. 2, (HA VII, 515–516.)

10. See below p. 156 ff.

11. This is a letter containing very general remarks of "wisdom" which Wilhelm receives as a kind of initiation rite.

12. *Lust* does not mean "lust," but rather "pleasure." There is no trace of lust in the entire novel.

13. Their names are never mentioned.

14. I am using "sentimental" here in Schiller's very restricted usage of the term. For Schiller, the sentimental person is one who has lost his immediate contact with nature and yearns for a restoration of this immediacy. According to Schiller, the lost contact with nature can never be recaptured.

Chapter Six

1. Not all refugees were poor and in need of help. In his *Campaign in France* Goethe describes the carriages of the wealthy refugees, which were loaded with goods and accompanied by many servants. But see my discussion of *Hermann and Dorothea* for the poor refugees.

2. According to the description of the costumes of the refugees, and to some other hints, their home must have been in the Alsace.

3.   And thus she entered the fields
that covered the back of the hill with its wide expanse.
She was still walking on her own ground,
Between fields she walked, along forests,
With the pear-tree in view . . . . (4th Book)

Chapter Seven

1. The German language, which distinguishes between the medieval, fortified castle (*Burg*) and the modern unfortified one (*Schloss*), makes the difference between the two castles of the Novelle perfectly clear.

2. Book II, beginning of chapter 5.

3. Book II, chapter 5.

Chapter Eight

1. One of the most delightful symbolic figures, expressing change, is the Greek god Proteus (*Faust II*, Act II) whose essence it is to change, and who takes Homunculus (see below p. 175 f) out into the sea, so that by the process of evolution he can be transformed into a man.

2. See Chapter II.

Chapter Nine

1. Goethe's art criticism and his publications on art had to be entirely disregarded here. The same is unfortunately true for his translations, as e.g. *The Life of Benvenuto Cellini*, or Diderot's *Neveu de Rameau*, etc.

2. *De l'Allemagne*, 1813. Part II, ch. VII. Madame de Staël, in the same part of the book, also devotes chs. XXI to XXIII to a discussion of Goethe's works.

Selected Bibliography

PRIMARY SOURCES

1. Collected Works (German only)

Werke, ed. im Auftrag der Grossherzogin Sophie von Sachsen. 133 vols. Weimar: Böhlau, 1887–1919. The most complete edition of Goethe's works, divided into four parts: 1. Works, 2. Scientific Writings, 3. Diaries, 4 Letters.

Gedenkausgabe der Werke, Briefe, Gespräche, ed. Ernst Beutler. Zürich: Artemis, 1948–55. 24 vols. A very thorough edition, with explanatory notes.

Goethes Werke. Hamburger Ausgabe in 14 Bänden, ed. Erich Trunz. Hamburg: Wegner, 1949 ff. This edition, while not complete, has extremely valuable introductions, commentaries and notes. The individual volumes are constantly being re-edited and the bibliographies kept up-to-date.

J. W. Goethe, *Sämtliche Werke* (dtv-*Gesamtausgabe*), ed. Peter Boerner (Munich: Deutscher Taschenbuch-Verlag, 1962 f.) 45 paperback volumes. The text used throughout is that established by Ernst Beutler for the Artemis edition.

2. Selected Recent English Translations

The Autobiography of Johann Wolfgang von Goethe, trans. by John Oxenford. New York: Horizon Press, 1969. A beautiful translation and an elegant book, with a fine introduction by Gregor Sebba.

Elective Affinities, transl. by Elizabeth Mayer and Louise Bogan. Chicago: Regnery, 1963. A very readable and fluid translation.

Faust I and *II,* transl. by Charles E. Passage. New York: Library of Liberal Arts, 1965. A faithful translation, preserving the rhythms and rhyme schemes of the original. Not perfect as a poetic work, but the only available complete translation.

Iphigenia in Tauris, transl. by John Prudhoe. New York: Barnes and Noble, 1966.

Iphigenia in Tauris, transl. by Charles E. Passage. New York: Ungar,

1963. Reprinted 1966. Has an interesting introduction on some ancient forms of the myth. A fine translation.

The Permanent Goethe, edited, selected, and with an introduction by Thomas Mann. New York: Dial Press, 1948. The volume contains *Faust I, Egmont, Iphigenie, The Sorrows of Young Werther,* excerpts from other prose works, and many well-chosen poems translated by a variety of authors.

The Sorrows of Young Werther, and Novella, transl. by Elizabeth Mayer and Louise Bogan. Foreword by W. H. Auden. New York: Random House, 1971.

Torquato Tasso, transl. by Charles E. Passage. New York: Ungar, 1966. A very successful translation.

3. Bibliographies

Pyritz, Hans Werner. *Goethe-Bibliographie,* Heidelberg: Winter, 1955–68, 2 vols.

Nicolai, Heinz. *Goethe Bibliographie,* Jahrbuch der Goethe-Gesellschaft 1952–53. "Neue Folge des Jahr-Buchs." This is a continuation of the Pyritz Bibliography which lags several years behind.

Dickson, Alexander J. *Goethe Bibliography in England, 1909–49, English Goethe Society Publications,* new series, vol. 19, 1949.

SECONDARY SOURCES

1. Critical Works—German

ALTHAUS, HORST, *Ästhetik, Ökonomie und Gesellschaft,* Berne: Francke, 1971. A sociological approach. Contains bibliography.

BEUTLER, ERNST. *Essays um Goethe.* Bremen: Schünemann, 1962. Not available in English. Valuable material for further research. Bibliography.

BOERNER, PETER. *Goethe* (Hamburg: Rowohlt, 1964). Vol. 100 of Rowohlt's Monographien.

BURCKHARDT, SIGURD. *The Drama of Language; Essays on Goethe and Kleist,* Baltimore: Johns Hopkins Press, 1970. Contains excellent essays on *Natürliche Tochter, Iphigenie* and *Tasso.*

Goethe-Handbuch. Goethe, seine Welt und Zeit in Welt und Wirkung, ed. Alfred Zastrau (Stuttgart: Metzler, 1961).

Götting, Franz. *Chronik von Goethes Leben* (Wiesbaden: Insel-Verlag, 1949). Reprinted as vol. 45 of the dtv edition listed above.

HELLER, ERICH. *Essays über Goethe,* Frankfurt: Insel, 1970. A collection in German of Heller's challenging essays.

JOCKERS, ERNST. *Mit Goethe* (Essays), Heidelberg: Winter, 1957. Contains the best statement on Goethe's relationship to nature.

STAIGER, EMIL. *Goethe,* Zürich: Artemis, 1949. 3 vols. The standard

German work on Goethe. Many of Staiger's views have been attacked in recent years.

STÖCKLEIN, PAUL. *Wege zum Späten Goethe.* Zweite neu bearbeitete und erweiterte Auflage. Hamburg: Schröder, 1960. Very sensitive with regard to the old Goethe.

2. Critical Works—English

ATKINS, STUART. *Goethe's "Faust"; A Literary Analysis.* Cambridge: Harvard University Press, 1958. The most complete and extensive interpretation of *Faust* in English. Indispensible. No bibliography.

BERGSTRAESSER, ARNOLD. *Goethe and the Modern Age* (Chicago: Regnery, 1950)

BRUFORD, W. H. *Culture and Society in Classical Weimar. 1775–1806.* London: Cambridge University Press, 1962. An excellent sociolocical study of Goethe's most active years in Weimar. Contains a bibliography.

CASSIRER, ERNST. *Rousseau, Kant, Goethe.* Hamden: Archon Books, 1961. Two fundamental essays.

FAIRLEY, BARKER. *A Study of Goethe.* Oxford: Clarendon Press, 1948. Still the best survey in English. No bibliography.

FRIEDENTHAL, RICHARD. *Goethe, His Life and Times.* London: Widenfeld and Nicolson, 1965. Includes "Bibliographical survey": 534–542. Written in a racy and irreverent style, it is a reliable and inexhaustible source of historical, biographical and sociological information.

GRAY, RONALD. *Goethe, A Critical Introduction.* London: Cambridge University Press, 1967. Slightly tinged by anthroposophy, but containing interesting material. Bibliography, pp. 271–273.

HATFIELD, HENRY. *Goethe, A Critical Introduction.* Cambridge: Harvard University Press, 1964. Identical with the paperback, called *Goethe, A Critical Guidebook.* New York: New Directions, 1963, by the same author. A broad, well-written introduction to Goethe's life and works.

LANGE, VICTOR, ed. *Goethe, A Collection of Critical Essays.* Englewood Cliffs: Prentice Hall, 1968. An excellent selection of recent English essays on various aspects of Goethe's work, with a fine introduction on Goethe's position in modern literature.

LEPPMANN, WOLFGANG. *The German Image of Goethe* (Oxford: Clarendon Press, 1961).

REISS, HANS. *Goethe's Novels.* London, 1969. A thorough and reliable discussion. (Select bibliography on pp. 288–301).

STRICH, FRITZ. *Goethe and World Literature* (London: Routledge & Kegan Paul, 1949).

VIETOR, KARL. *Goethe, the Poet* (Cambridge, Mass.: Harvard University Press, 1949).

WILKINSON, ELIZABETH M. and WILLOUGHBY, L.A., *Goethe, Poet and Thinker*. London: Arnold, 1962. A collection of essays by two renowned English scholars on a variety of topics—all interesting and challenging.

Index

Index